100 THINGS INDIANS FANS SHOULD KNOW & DO BEFORE THEY DIE

Zack Meisel

Library of Congress Cataloging-in-Publication Data

Meisel, Zack, 1989-
100 things Indians fans should know & do before they die / Zack Meisel.
pages cm
ISBN 978-1-62937-032-3
1. Cleveland Indians (Baseball team)—History. 2. Cleveland Indians (Baseball team)—Miscellanea. I. Title. II. Title: One hundred things Indians fans should know and do before they die.
GV875.C7M45 2015
796.357'640977132—dc23
2014041807

This book is available in quantity at special discounts for your group or organization. For further information, contact:

Triumph Books LLC
814 North Franklin Street
Chicago, Illinois 60610
(312) 337-0747
www.triumphbooks.com

Printed in U.S.A.
ISBN: 978-1-62937-032-3
Design by Patricia Frey
Photos courtesy of Getty Images unless otherwise indicated

For my late father, Jeff, and for my late grandmother, Joyce, who only had an interest in baseball and in the Indians because her grandson was writing about those topics. We couldn't even begin a meal at the hole-in-the-wall Chinese food joint near her house without her flooding my brain with story ideas, most of them outrageous and unrealistic and all of them appreciated. I'm sure she would have contributed every thought she could muster as I composed this book.

And for my mother, Wendy, who has forever begged me to acknowledge her baseball acumen, which she claims rivals that of any other mother. If only this were a book about Don Mattingly or Greg Maddux.

Contents

Foreword

I wish I would have been good enough as a player to have played at this level, but I wasn't. So for me, becoming the radio announcer for the Indians was the next-best thing to being a major league player. There are only 30 of these jobs and I was one of the lucky ones who got one of the 30. The odds of that aren't very good for a guy who grew up on a dairy farm in Wisconsin.

Listening to Milwaukee Braves games and then the Brewers when I was growing up, this job seemed like the impossible dream but it became a reality. I can't quite get over the fact that it really happened. From a professional standpoint, the Cleveland Indians mean everything to me. I can't think of a better organization to have worked for. We can't think of a better city to have raised our four children. We came here with a two-month-old and now have four children and we never had any thoughts of going anywhere else. We had other opportunities, but never seriously considered them because we thought that much of the organization and the city.

I know how blessed we have been to get this opportunity and to have witnessed a ballpark that helped revitalize a city, a ballclub that ended all of the national jokes about Cleveland. You think of this ballpark and those teams in the '90s—that was the end of late-night talk shows taking shots at Cleveland. It ended it. To have seen all of those great moments and the great Hall of Fame players who have played here, I've been really blessed.

You never know how fans are going to take you. I think I was really fortunate that I worked with Herb Score for eight years, since Herb was such an icon. Because Herb accepted me, that opened the door for fans to accept me. It was very fortuitous to be able to work with Herb.

You want to work in a city where the fans care. The worst thing is apathy. Florida has great weather. So do California and Atlanta. But in a lot of those places, those people didn't grow up with those teams. They moved to those cities, so they may be fans, but they don't live and die with it like they do here in Cleveland and some of the other Midwest cities.

I always wanted to live in the Midwest, as did my wife. We wanted to raise a family in the Midwest because we believe in those values. But also, the fans care so much. If fans care, it can't help but make you be a better broadcaster. You may have a bad season, but you know how much they care for that night's game.

This job has given us a great life. We owe everything to baseball. The home we live in, the ability to send our kids to college—we owe all of that to baseball. Outside of my family, nothing means more to me than what the Indians have meant.

—Tom Hamilton

Introduction

I was eight years old, a third-grader at Parkside Elementary School with few interests other than playing outside, watching *Hey Arnold!*, eating chicken fingers, and following the Cleveland Indians. I had no idea that one of those hobbies—not the chicken fingers—would provide the fuel for the activity that eventually became my career.

On April 15, 1998, the Indians hosted the Seattle Mariners at Jacobs Field. In the third inning, menacing Mariners southpaw Randy Johnson buzzed a fastball near the head of Tribe leadoff man Kenny Lofton. Tempers flared, benches cleared and, temporarily, cooler heads prevailed. Johnson returned to the mound. Lofton settled back into the batter's box. And then it happened again. Johnson fired a heater in nearly the same location. The benches cleared again and both players were ejected.

I had never seen anything like it. I witnessed the Indians' World Series misstep six months earlier and the theatrical journey they traveled to arrive at that point. But I had never seen this element of the game, one with so much attitude and passion. At school the next day, I wanted to discuss the events with my friends and classmates, but they were more intent on learning multiplication or watching *Bill Nye the Science Guy*. So, I wrote about it. I recapped what I had watched unfold. In a way, it was a third-grader penning a game story, a type of writing I would repeat hundreds of times later on in my life. I wasn't assigned to write anything. I just wanted to. A handful of years later, when I felt the urge to take a high school journalism class, that sequence appeared in my mind. I wasn't aware at the time, but even as a little kid, I wanted to be a sportswriter. Of course, accepting the fact that my 72-mph fastball wouldn't cut it in the big leagues certainly helped me reach that conclusion a bit more swiftly.

When I was asked to write this book, the task seemed somewhat surreal at first. Eight-year-old me would have been just as eager to attack it as I was when I actually received the inquiry. A native Clevelander, I grew up during the golden era of Indians baseball. For the first part of my life, sellout crowds, household names, and memorable Octobers were all I knew. I was spoiled. Still, it never really seemed crazy that I ended up covering the Indians. It just felt right. And to write a book about their history just reinforced the connection I have had with the team since my childhood.

I have had the opportunity to interview and get to know many of the players, coaches, and executives I grew up idolizing. Those relationships are quite different now; I don't wear my youth-large Jim Thome T-shirt when I interview him. Now, it's no big deal to sit in Robbie Alomar's suite at the Rogers Centre in Toronto and ask him about his relationship with his brother. Sandy Alomar Jr. and I have spent hours reminiscing about his magical 1997 season and analyzing why his little brother always picks up the tab when they share a meal.

The main thing I have learned during my years covering the Indians is that many who have spent a decent amount of time in the organization will speak passionately about it. The Indians were a charter member of the American League in 1901. Since then, there is enough history to fill thousands of pages. Speaking to current and former players and coaches and front-office bigwigs about the more than 100 years of moments and memories and personalities has been a privilege. To an eight-year-old in April 1998, the Johnson-Lofton feud was the most essential event in franchise history, but in reality, it's just one tiny, tiny blip on the radar. Here are 100 of those more pressing and memorable moments, personalities, events, and activities.

1 The Rebirth of the Franchise

The Indians were set to host an open house at newly minted Jacobs Field on April 3, 1994, a Sunday afternoon. It snowed. The event was canceled.

It was not the most promising omen for the grand opening of a new ballpark set to happen the next day.

The Friday before Opening Day, the Indians dedicated a statue to Hall of Fame pitcher Bob Feller outside of Gate C, out beyond center field. A day later, the Indians and Pirates squared off in an exhibition game intended to serve as a test for ballpark operations. Fans poured into the stadium until it was packed to near capacity.

The open house was supposed to give fans who didn't have tickets to Saturday's affair a chance to explore the new building. Mother Nature, however, refused to cooperate. Fortunately for the team, Opening Day brought sunny skies, albeit with chilly temperatures. It was 48 degrees at first pitch.

"People were so excited and they were wide-eyed, their jaws dropped, smiling and thanking us," said Bob DiBiasio, Indians senior vice president of public affairs. "They were in awe that this was theirs. It was a real badge of honor for people in our town to say, 'This is mine. This is ours. I'm so proud to call this my ballpark.'"

Just how much better was Cleveland's new venue compared to old Municipal Stadium? Mark Shapiro, then the club's director of minor league operations, was overseeing the end of minor league spring training in Winter Haven, Florida, so he could not attend the opener at Jacobs Field. Instead, he and player development advisor Johnny Goryl ventured to a local Beef 'O' Brady's and requested that management find the game on TV.

"It was a major cultural shift, not just for the fans, but for us," Shapiro said. "We went from a weight room that was basically a crowbar and three sets of dumbbells in the corner of the training room to a state of the art weight room. We went from a kitchen that was one refrigerator with a jar of peanut butter and a jar of jelly and a loaf of bread on top of the fridge to an incredible kitchen.

"When you look at the training, the fueling, the development of our athletes, we went from prehistoric to state of the art, cutting edge. It wasn't a subtle jump. It was a dramatic jump."

And its debut received a dramatic amount of attention.

DiBiasio escorted President Bill Clinton around the ballpark that day. Clinton tossed out the ceremonial first pitch. Draped in a blue Indians windbreaker and blue Tribe hat with a red brim, he wore a light brown mitt on his right hand as he heaved a baseball down the middle to catcher Sandy Alomar Jr. Ohio Governor George Voinovich and Feller followed with ceremonial first pitches of their own.

The Indians had planned for this day. They rebuilt their roster, devoting long, trying years to developing young players. When that green talent started to blossom, they cashed in on the free-agent market and pieced together a group that they felt could contend, all right as the organization opened the doors on a brand new ballpark. The endeavor culminated in that Monday afternoon. All the hard work and pain suffered through decades of losing, the long, miserable nights at a massive, mostly empty stadium—it was all set to dissipate in favor of a new era, one Cleveland hoped would be rife with triumph and glory.

And then Seattle Mariners pitcher Randy Johnson held the Tribe hitless through the first seven innings of the first game.

Alomar finally ended Johnson's bid at an Opening Day no-hitter with a single to right field with no outs in the eighth. The base

President Bill Clinton throws out the ceremonial first pitch on Opening Day 1994 before the Indians and Mariners squared off. It was the first-ever game at Jacobs Field.

Ballpark Firsts

Plenty of history has been made at the corner of Carnegie and Ontario, where Progressive Field, then named Jabobs Field, opened in 1994. The ballpark's firsts include the following:

First pitch: President Bill Clinton on April 4, 1994

Actual pitch: Dennis Martinez on April 4, 1994

Hit: Seattle Mariners outfielder Eric Anthony, a home run, on April 4, 1994

Home run: Anthony on April 4, 1994

Hit by an Indian: Sandy Alomar on April 4, 1994

Home run by an Indian: Eddie Murray on April 7, 1994

Grand slam: Paul Sorrento on May 9, 1995

Inside-the-park home run: David Bell off of Seattle's Randy Johnson on April 15, 1998

No-hitter: Angels right-hander Ervin Santana on July 27, 2011

Triple play: Casey Blake to Asdrubal Cabrera to Victor Martinez on August 27, 2007

Unassisted triple play: Asdrubal Cabrera on May 12, 2008

knock came after Feller, the only pitcher in major league history to toss a no-no on Opening Day, broke into the ESPN TV booth and attempted to jinx Johnson on air. Alomar's hit moved Candy Maldonado, who had walked, to second. Both runners advanced a base on a wild pitch and Manny Ramirez brought them home with a double off the wall in left field to tie the game.

The matinee extended to extra innings and both teams plated a run in the 10th. In the 11th, the Indians christened their new home with a fitting finale to its first affair. Reserve outfielder Wayne Kirby slapped a two-out single to left field off of Seattle reliever Kevin King. Eddie Murray scored from third and the Indians celebrated.

The Indians would take an immediate liking to their new residence. They won a franchise-record 18 consecutive home games from May 13–June 19 in their inaugural year at Jacobs Field. The club had the best home record in the league in 1994, at 35–16. Of course, it all began with that Monday afternoon. What a fortuitous finish and a proper culmination to everything the organization had worked toward.

"I would contend that that was the singular most important day in franchise history," DiBiasio said. "It provided us the ability to carry forward, where if this thing is not built, we're gone. There is no baseball in Cleveland."

2 A Long Time Coming

September 8, 1995, was akin to Christmas in Cleveland. Call it "Clinchmas." You know presents will reside under the tree, but it's still exciting to first spot them. The Indians knew their division title was inevitable in '95, but celebrating the capturing of the playoff berth still proved to be a joyous occasion.

The Indians won 100 games in 1995, a strike-shortened season that limited teams to 144 contests. They outscored their opponents by nearly two runs per game, finishing 14 games ahead of any other American League team and 30 games ahead of the second-best finisher in their division, the Kansas City Royals. Cleveland led the American League in runs, hits, home runs, stolen bases, batting average, on-base percentage, slugging percentage and total bases. Indians hitters struck out less frequently than any other offense, while the pitching staff's ERA was nearly a half-run better than that of any other AL staff. They issued the fewest number of free passes and recorded the third-most strikeouts.

Jason Giambi was a rookie infielder for the Oakland Athletics in 1995. They went 0–7 against the Indians that season.

"If you could go into Cleveland and play well, you knew what kind of ballclub you had," Giambi said, "because they were so good and so stacked that if you could play with them, you had a good team."

The Indians finished at least nine games over the .500 mark in each full month of the regular season. Their worst showing came in July, when they posted an 18–9 mark. They didn't slow down in August or September, when the division title was all but a guarantee. The players wanted to out-do one another. They sought bragging rights within the clubhouse. They didn't want to stop. The hunger to exceed their own standards and those of their peers drove them to new heights.

"That's why you win by 30 games," said Bob DiBiasio, Indians senior vice president of public affairs.

The Indians sat at 85–37 on September 8. They gripped a commanding 22½-game lead in the division. That Friday evening, they hosted the Baltimore Orioles in a series-opening affair. An eager group of 41,656—a sellout crowd, of course—filled Jacobs Field, knowing what was likely to come after nine triumphant innings. In the third inning, Omar Vizquel opened the scoring with a sacrifice fly. Eddie Murray followed three batters later with a two-run single. Cleveland coasted from there. Orel Hershiser didn't need any more backing. The back end of the Tribe bullpen—Paul Assenmacher, Julian Tavarez and Jose Mesa, who earned his 40th save—cruised through the final frames.

As Jim Thome straddled third base, waiting—for eons, seemingly—for Jeff Huson's two-out pop-up to descend from the stratosphere and fall into his glove, fans shrieked with excitement.

Thome squeezed the division-clinching out in his glove, kept his left arm raised and dashed to the mob scene at the center of the diamond. Indians coaches embraced in the home dugout as fireworks exploded high above the outfield. The players dumped a cooler of Gatorade onto manager Mike Hargrove.

Radio announcer Tom Hamilton shouted: "The season of dreams has become a reality. Cleveland: You will have an October to remember!"

It marked the earliest any team in the divisional play era had clinched a postseason berth. It marked the Indians' first ticket to October in 41 years. It marked a new beginning for a franchise that had suffered through decades of ineptitude.

The team raised a flag after the game to signify its accomplishment. Kenny Lofton was granted the honor of pulling it, as Garth Brooks' "The Dance" played on the ballpark sound system, a request called in by Hargrove. It was the favorite song of Steve Olin, the Indians relief pitcher who died—along with teammate Tim Crews—in a tragic boating accident just two years earlier. As the Indians paid tribute on this momentous evening, tears streamed down the players' faces.

Looking back on the memory of
The dance we shared 'neath the stars above
For a moment all the world was right
How could I have known that you'd ever say goodbye
And now I'm glad I didn't know
The way it all would end, the way it all would go
Our lives are better left to chance, I could have missed the pain
But I'd have had to miss the dance

Upon clinching a playoff spot, the front office received congratulatory phone calls from former players, including Gary Bell,

Max Alvis, Duane Kuiper, and Pat Tabler. Former Cleveland Browns head coach Sam Rutigliano wrote the team a note that read: "Wonderful job knocking the town on its ear."

"Right then, you thought, 'This is blown up,'" DiBiasio said. "Just pure joy. There is no joy in doing things by yourself. The joy comes in working as a team and achieving success. You're able to turn to your buddy and have big hugs and tears. Just, 'Wow. We did it. We're here. We're legit.'"

For former shortstop Omar Vizquel, it's a feat only appreciated more with time: "You don't realize what kind of team and what kind of teammates you have until you see it now from where we are. You look back and say, 'Wow, those guys were amazing. We had one of the greatest teams ever.'"

3 A Year to Remember

The Indians had everything in 1948. They had three starting pitchers with at least 19 wins: Bob Lemon (20), Gene Bearden (20), and Bob Feller (19). They had hitters who produced sparkling offensive numbers: Joe Gordon (32 home runs, 124 RBIs), Lou Boudreau (.355 average, 18 home runs, 106 RBIs), Ken Keltner (.297 average, 31 home runs, 119 RBIs), Larry Doby (.301 average, 14 home runs), and Dale Mitchell (.336 average, 204 hits).

Cleveland had three players (Boudreau, Gordon, Keltner) in the All-Star Game starting lineup and two more (Lemon, Feller) on the pitching staff. They had a player/manager (Boudreau) who also captured the American League MVP award and had plenty of motivation. Owner Bill Veeck had planned to trade Boudreau during the previous offseason before rumors swirled and

The Funeral

When the Indians were mathematically eliminated from the pennant race in 1949, owner Bill Veeck captained a funeral for their status as world champions, acquired when they won the World Series the previous year.

They folded up the pennant flag and buried it in a coffin. Player/manager Lou Boudreau, his coaching staff and several front-office executives served as pallbearers. They placed the coffin into a hearse, which Veeck drove around the field at Cleveland Municipal Stadium. The players joined in on the ceremony as the team nestled the coffin into a grave in center field.

The Indians finished the 1949 campaign with an 89–65 record, good for third place in the American League.

overwhelming backlash convinced him to keep him. They also had a landmark midseason addition in Satchel Paige, a legend in the Negro Leagues who contributed to Cleveland's stout pitching staff down the stretch.

The Indians topped their opponents by five or more runs on 43 occasions. Tribe hurlers tossed 26 shutouts. It was a complete team, one that jockeyed with the New York Yankees and Boston Red Sox for American League supremacy throughout the summer. The Indians spent about half the season in first place. They never held a lead larger than 3½ games and never trailed by more than 4½ games. Facing their most daunting deficit with only three weeks remaining in the regular season, they rattled off a pair of seven-game winning streaks in September to erase the gap.

Cleveland held a two-game lead entering the final series against the Detroit Tigers at Municipal Stadium. The Indians sent their three-headed monster of Lemon, Bearden, and Feller to the mound, but the Tigers took two of three to force the Tribe into a one-game playoff with the Red Sox. The winner would advance to the World Series to face the Boston Braves.

Bearden started the playoff game, despite twirling a complete-game shutout just two days earlier. He logged another nine innings against the Sox, as Boudreau socked a pair of home runs and the Indians proceeded to their first Fall Classic in nearly three decades with an 8–3 triumph.

The Indians captured the championship in six games, clinching the series at Braves Field. It was a series dominated by pitching; in only one game (Game 5) did either team score more than four runs. Bearden relieved Lemon in the eighth inning of Game 6 to close out the decisive victory, as the Indians recorded the second championship in franchise history.

4 Filling the Seats

On a cluster of pillars in right field reside the names and retired numbers of Bob Feller, Larry Doby, Bob Lemon, Earl Averill, Lou Boudreau, Mel Harder and Jackie Robinson. On an adjacent wall rests one other retired number, perhaps the most cherished in Indians lore. It reads: "455: The Fans."

From June 12, 1995, to April 4, 2001, Indians fans filled Jacobs Field to capacity. The club established a Major League Baseball record with 455 consecutive sellouts. It became the first team in the league to sell every ticket to every game for an entire season. It did that for five straight years.

The Red Sox eventually topped the Indians' sellout streak in 2008, but Cleveland's stretch will never be forgotten near Lake Erie. The Colorado Rockies had owned the league's longest streak, at 203 games, before the Indians bested that mark.

"The convergence of things that resulted in 455 consecutive sellouts is a miracle," said Bob DiBiasio, Indians senior vice president of public affairs. "People just don't truly understand. It never happened in the history of baseball. Not once."

On June 7, 1995, 36,363 watched the Indians top the Tigers in 10 innings on a Jim Thome walk-off home run. For nearly six years thereafter, every green seat and silver metal bench in the ballpark was occupied. Jacobs Field was a new entity, a shiny new toy in the forefront of the downtown landscape. Fans were going to flock to the building for a while anyway. Then, the realization of the team's potential began to spread.

"As that talent on the field started to be more and more evident to our fans, they started to feed off of it," said team president Mark Shapiro. "The packed houses were no longer here just to see a new ballpark. They were here to see one of the best teams in baseball in one of the nicest ballparks in baseball. It just became an incredible amount of civic pride bubbling over in a combination of what was a crown jewel building with a team that they were proud of."

The lineup included a litany of All-Star caliber players: Kenny Lofton, Carlos Baerga, Albert Belle, Manny Ramirez, Sandy Alomar Jr., and Thome. Those talents boasted flamboyance, flair, and swagger, and they backed it up on the diamond. Fans lined up to partake in that powerful aura.

"Their offense was unreal, with Thome, Manny, Alomar, Kenny, all of them," said Indians center fielder Michael Bourn. "Everybody knew about them in the '90s."

The attraction was evident to even the visitors. Shapiro can recall the honking horns from cars mired in traffic on the streets of downtown Cleveland after each game, the dominance of the Indians' potent lineup, and the intimidation and fear the group instilled in opposing pitchers.

"It was the place to go," said Jason Giambi, a rookie infielder for the Oakland Athletics in 1995. "It was unbelievable. They were selling out every game. Some of the best players in the game were playing there. The fans were coming out in droves, The Flats, that city was bumping. It was fun to play there."

People wanted to watch them on the road, too. Former Indians closer Chris Perez was raised near Tampa Bay, Florida. He can remember venturing to Tropicana Field to watch Thome and Ramirez and David Justice launch home runs against the hometown Devil Rays.

"People would come in here knowing, 'All right, we're going to get our ass kicked,'" DiBiasio said. "It was that simple. And then when the Tribe came to their city, it was, 'Oh shit. Let's see if we can get one out of these guys this weekend, because they're going to beat the devil out of our pitching.'"

Jacobs Field, pictured at full capacity. Between June 12, 1995, and April 4, 2001, the Indians established a Major League Baseball record with 455 consecutive sellouts.

The star power was signed or drafted and then developed in the Indians' system at the start of the run. As time elapsed, however, the Indians employed one of the league's highest payrolls—a benefit of the new ballpark, the height of the fan interest, and the newfound success. Shapiro compared the organization to the Los Angeles Dodgers and Boston Red Sox. He said the club's ability to impact the free-agent market and operate differently from most of the league was "incredible."

"They had the perfect pieces of the puzzle," Giambi said. "They had homegrown guys, free agents, Thome and these guys. Albert Belle left and they brought in David Justice. They would just replace one piece of the puzzle with another. It was just unbelievable to watch. One free agent would leave and they would bring somebody else in or a kid would take over. It was pretty special."

To amass a record number of sellouts required a perfect storm of sorts, an unforeseen confluence of variables that garnered the team such an unheralded, dedicated following. The economy was thriving: people had disposable income available to spend on the various costs incurred when attending a game. The city's NFL franchise had relocated: owner Art Modell moved the Browns to Baltimore after the 1995 season.

At the time the Indians opened the doors to their new establishment in April 1994, they had a talented crop of young players that was prepared to contend for the postseason. The timing worked wonders. The fans caught on quickly.

"It was the coolest thing," DiBiasio said. "Our guys knew. That energy building up, from about 3 o'clock on. Three hours before games, people just started lining up. Kids played catch on the grass.

"A remarkable set of circumstances came together with a team with such sparkle. This team was dynamic."

From the time Jacobs Field opened in 1994 until the end of the streak, the club sold out 95 percent of its regular season games. The Indians eclipsed the Rockies' sellout record on September 9,

1997. They attracted more than 19 million fans to the ballpark during the streak. When it began, the Indians had played the first two months of what would be their first playoff season in more than four decades. The club qualified for the postseason for five consecutive years, but when it fell one game short in 2000, ticket sales suffered. Fans packed the stadium for Opening Day in 2001, but the second game of the season featured a crowd of only 32,763, about three-fourths full. The sight of empty green seats had not existed for 2,122 days.

"We want to celebrate that as probably the single-greatest juncture in modern Indians baseball," Shapiro said. "So we want to absolutely celebrate that. We've done that around the ballpark. We've done that by bringing back players. We've done that by continuing to celebrate the players that made up those teams and those will always be a part of who we are as a team and an organization that we're very proud of."

It is, however, the standard by which all Indians teams and eras are now measured. On April 22, 2001, less than three weeks after the sellout streak was snapped, the Indians unveiled the red letters and numbers on the pillar in the right-field mezzanine. No one will ever again don the numbers worn by Feller, Lemon, Harder, Doby, Boudreau, Averill, or Robinson. And, in all likelihood, no era of Indians baseball will spark the long-term, widespread fanaticism that the teams from 1994–2001 did.

"The most difficult barometer for us is being measured by the '90s," DiBiasio said. "It's so difficult for the franchise to have to live up to that and be measured by it, but that's our goal.

"Our goal is to turn the town upside down like we did then."

5 The Pinnacle of Heartbreak

The champagne was prepped to be popped. The Most Valuable Player trophy was etched and ready to be awarded. The walls of the visitor's clubhouse were draped with plastic to control the unshakeable tradition of spraying bubbly.

It all unfolded so quickly, so shockingly, so painfully for the Indians.

Every so often, Sandy Alomar Jr. receives a phone call. His friends will inform him when a replay of Game 7 of the 1997 World Series between the Indians and the Florida Marlins is on TV. He will not watch it.

"Let me know when it's on when the ending changes," he tells them.

After the Indians forced the decisive affair with a win in Game 6, radio announcer Tom Hamilton joined vice president of public relations Bob DiBiasio and his wife, Penny, in South Beach to celebrate. Hamilton said they were the only people in Miami who even knew the World Series was taking place.

"That's when you knew how different it was," Hamilton said. "You knew back in Cleveland the town was going wild."

The state of emotions would reverse course pretty quickly.

Anyone involved in the game can remember the date: October 26. They can remember how Tribe skipper Mike Hargrove—who was celebrating his 48th birthday—opted to start the kid, Jaret Wright, instead of the grizzled veteran workhorse, Charles Nagy. They can still envision the raucous crowd of 67,204 at Pro Player Stadium. Years later, Wright remembers everything about the entire series.

"What I ate, what I was thinking, the whole deal," he said.

Mark Shapiro, then the Indians' director of minor league operations, had moved out of his seat to the portal behind home plate, where he watched the events unfold with special assistant Bud Black. Shapiro said he felt constant jitters, even after Tony Fernandez supplied Cleveland with a 2–0 lead on a two-run single in the third inning. He felt unrelenting knots in his stomach as Bobby Bonilla sliced into the Indians' advantage with a solo home run on Wright's first offering of the seventh.

"It just exponentially increased to the point that you were just sick to your stomach," Shapiro said. "Especially with how it ended. It was just incredibly deflating to go through that range of emotions in such a short period of time."

The Indians carried a 2–1 edge into the ninth. League figureheads had initiated the proper postgame preparations. Indians players, coaches, and executives were on the top dugout step, ready to spill out onto the field and commence a celebration not experienced by a professional Cleveland franchise since 1964.

"The feeling that we had in Game 7 of the '97 World Series, sitting at the edge of the dugout, waiting for the explosion of the players to go out and celebrate on the field and just thinking what that would have meant to generations of Indians fans, we think about it all the time," DiBiasio said. "We got so damn close to bringing that to reality and that's all we do is continue to work hard to try to get to that point to make it real.

"You really have a sense of how difficult it really is to win."

Singles by Moises Alou and Charles Johnson gave the Marlins runners at the corners with one out against Tribe closer Jose Mesa. Craig Counsell followed with a sacrifice fly that lured right fielder Manny Ramirez toward the warning track. Florida had tied the game. Mesa had blown the save.

"You could feel the momentum start to shift a little bit," Hargrove said.

League bigwigs had to remove Chad Ogea's name from the MVP trophy. The Indians had to resist the temptation to permit the deflating feeling from swallowing them whole. There was still baseball to play. The game proceeded into extra innings.

"It's a scar that never goes away," Alomar said. "You play in two World Series and have a chance to win them, but Game 7—anything could have won that game. It does bother me."

In the bottom of the 11th, with Nagy on the hill, Bonilla opened the frame with a single. The right-hander retired Gregg Zaun, but Counsell hit a grounder that scooted under Fernandez's glove. The miscue by the typically sure-handed fielder placed runners on the corners with one out. Nagy intentionally walked Jim Eisenreich and got Devon White to tap into a force out at the plate. It all came together in the Marlins having the bases loaded with two outs. Edgar Renteria then lined a series-winning base hit that skimmed off the tip of Nagy's glove and shot into center field. Counsell scored and Cleveland suffered.

"It was bad," Alomar said. "We're scarred for life. It still, to this day, bothers me. I was sad that we couldn't pull it out. I got over it when we had more games, but that was one of the biggest missions we had here, to win a World Series, and we didn't."

The Indians boasted a championship contender each year from 1994–2001. They never came closer to the ultimate triumph than they did in 1997. Hell, no team can come closer than that without actually capturing the crown.

"I told them to be proud of themselves," Hargrove said, "they're a good ball club, that they played a good series and they had a very good postseason and there's no reason for them to feel ashamed or sad or anything. Feel the loss, but don't feel bad about who they are and where they've come from and where they've gone. They should feel proud of themselves. I told them to keep their heads high because they were champions. They were winners."

6 Rapid Robert

Mark Shapiro had settled in to his new office at the Indians' spring training complex in Tucson, Arizona, when he heard a noise.

Thump. Thump. Thump.

Shapiro's office shared a wall with the outfield at Hi Corbett Field and it sounded as though someone was throwing a ball against the cinder block. Shapiro, then an assistant in the baseball operations department, walked outside to check. Sure enough, there was 73-year-old Bob Feller chucking a baseball over and over.

Feller spent his entire 18-year career with the Indians. He hung around the club long after his playing days, wore a Tribe cap into the Baseball Hall of Fame upon his induction in 1962, and has a permanent seat in the Progressive Field press box.

"I think he's one of the great players in the history of the game," Shapiro said, "and for him to play his career here and do what he did off the field, too, was pretty remarkable."

Feller amassed 266 wins, the most of any pitcher in franchise history. He won 20 or more games six times. He led the league in strikeouts on seven occasions and tallied a career-high 348 in 1946, the seventh-most in any season in the modern era. He led the league in innings pitched five times. He made eight All-Star teams, logged 279 complete games, and tossed three no-hitters (including the only one ever on Opening Day) and 12 one-hitters. He fanned 15 in his first career start as a 17-year-old and 2,581 in all. Feller blew away batters with his blazing fastball, an asset that earned him national recognition and buzz: magazine covers, radio coverage, and a competition in which he threw the pitch while a motorcycle whizzed by at full speed. He finished in the top five in balloting for Most Valuable Player four times.

Yet perhaps what Feller is most respected for is his military service and his unabashed willingness to serve his country. Feller enlisted in the Navy in 1941 and spent four years as an anti-aircraft gunner aboard the U.S.S. Alabama. He was the first major leaguer to enlist, a leader, a trendsetter, a trailblazer. The Japanese bombed Pearl Harbor on December 7, 1941. The next day, Feller placed his budding baseball career on hold and joined the Navy. He earned six campaign ribbons and eight battle stars, but he also refused commendation for his efforts.

He is known for his quote: "I'm no hero. Heroes don't come back. Survivors return home."

"Over time, having a lot of conversations with him," Shapiro said, "he was also a guy that the more you talk to him, the more you were impressed by what a strong man he was. He was an impressive person."

To honor Feller's service and selflessness and those who follow in his footsteps in their own way, the Indians created the Bob Feller Act of Valor Award in 2013. The distinction recognizes three individuals who reflect the values, integrity, and dedication to serving the country that Feller also possessed. The award is presented annually to one U.S. Navy Chief Petty Officer, one member of the Baseball Hall of Fame, and one active major leaguer.

"It was instituted so we could continue to educate people on service above self, the greatest generation of service men and women, making sure people understand their sacrifices and how that can't be lost on the younger generation," said Bob DiBiasio, Indians senior vice president of public affairs. "Bob was right in the middle of that. He was the first to stand up. He had a deferment coming his way that he said no to. They were going to put him on the mainland in some capacity and he said, 'No. Put me on a boat in the middle of the Pacific, right in the heat of battle.' There were 500 people in professional baseball who did that, but he was the first."

Former Indians designated hitter Travis Hafner, who spoke to Feller on occasion during the Hall of Famer's annual spring training visits, spoke highly of Feller's choice to serve instead of pitch.

"He didn't do anything half-hearted," Hafner said. "He put everything he had into what he did and he had his beliefs that he believed in. He was a very strong man."

When clearing out the Bob Feller Museum in Feller's hometown of Van Meter, Iowa, DiBiasio discovered a Western Union telegraph sent to Feller from Jackie Robinson, who congratulated the hurler on being inducted into the Hall of Fame and expressed how honored he was to share that ceremony with him in 1962. Robinson and Feller, along with Bill McKechnie, elected by the Veterans' Committee, were the only inductees that year.

The Indians honored Feller in 1994 with a statue erected outside of the brand new Jacobs Field. In his later years, he spent every game in the third row in the press box, in the section closest to the door and the seat closest to home plate. After his death in 2010, the Indians placed a memorial of sorts on the desk at that seat, which will never again be occupied.

"His whole life," DiBiasio said, "he probably was one of the greatest ambassadors of the game of baseball there ever was around the world and he did so as a Cleveland Indian."

When considering the lengthy history of the Cleveland franchise, which dates back to 1901, perhaps no name better represents the organization than Feller.

"Without question," DiBiasio said. "He was a man who committed his life to the city of Cleveland and to the one team. He performed at a Hall of Fame level. I don't see how you could say there's anyone else. He is the singular name. He is the true face of our franchise."

7 Little Lake Nellie

The Olins lived across the hall from the DiBiasios in an apartment building in Winter Haven, Florida, where the Indians held spring training beginning in 1993. Steve Olin was the closer on a young team that was finally jelling. Bob DiBiasio was the vice president of public relations of an organization that was finally heading in the right direction. Their wives had become close. Steve and Patti had 7-month-old twins, Garrett and Kaylee. Patti could not give both a bottle at the same time, so Penny DiBiasio would venture across the hall and lend a hand at 11:00 PM each night.

The Indians had one day off in the spring of 1993. The Dodgers had offered to make up a rained-out affair that day, but manager Mike Hargrove declined, knowing it would not sit well with his players. The DiBiasios spent that day at Disney World, about a 40-minute trek northeast. Bob's parents joined him, Penny, and their young children, Patrick and Julie. Bob was carrying Julie and Penny was carrying Patrick as they returned to their residence shortly after 11:00 PM. Penny turned to Bob and said: "Something is wrong. The kids aren't crying next door. It's feeding time. They aren't crying."

Penny placed Patrick in his crib. Bob rested Julie in her crib. Penny walked over to the answering machine. Bob sat down and turned the TV to ESPN. As the lead story came across—something about an accident involving players on the Indians—Bob could hear his wife bawling her eyes out in the bedroom. The team doctor had left voicemails begging Bob to call him immediately.

Steve Olin and fellow reliever Tim Crews had died in a boating accident. Pitcher Bobby Ojeda had been injured.

Charles Nagy, the All-Star pitcher, and his wife, Jackie, came running up to the Olins' apartment. They noticed the DiBiasios had not even bothered to shut their door upon arriving back home, so they joined Bob and Penny. Eventually, eight or nine people sat in the apartment, unrelenting tears pouring down everyone's faces.

DiBiasio called general manager John Hart. They agreed to meet at the team's offices at 4:30 AM to map out what they needed to do.

"The goofy part is, you sit there and you go, 'You have to go to work,'" DiBiasio said. "'You have to get a clear head. You have work to do and people are counting on you to do the right thing.'"

They held a morning press conference. They planned to hold one every few hours to keep the public informed and to prevent reporters from scavenging for information. First, Hart and Hargrove addressed the media. Then, Hargrove met with the team as players filed in for what would have been a regular game day. Some players had no idea what had happened.

"There were guys who came in the clubhouse that morning," DiBiasio said, "and saw all the TV trucks and said, 'Wow, did we make a trade? What the heck is going on here?' Then they walk in and see everybody crying and talking to one another."

DiBiasio approached second baseman Carlos Baerga, an All-Star the year before and one of the team's leaders, to represent the players. Nagy could not bring himself to do it. He and his wife were close with the Olins. Baerga, though, agreed. He spoke on behalf of his teammates. Later, the entire bullpen sat through a press conference. Finally, Sharon Hargrove, the manager's wife, talked Patti into sitting before the media with a few of the other wives. In all, the team held four press conferences.

"It was horrific," DiBiasio said.

Crews had wanted to throw a party at his ranch. He was the new guy in the bullpen after he spent the first six years of his big league career with the Dodgers. The Olins had trouble finding their way to the Crews' residence on Little Lake Nellie in Clermont, Florida, about 40 miles north of Winter Haven. They did not have the benefit of a GPS or a cell phone. At one point, Patti pleaded with her husband to turn around. Steve could call Tim from the apartment and apologize. They would see each other the next day anyway. Steve, though, forged ahead. He was the captain of the bullpen, the last line of defense in the ninth inning of every winnable game. Crews was the new guy. Steve felt a sense of responsibility in getting to know him.

In the aftermath of the accident, the Florida Fish and Wildlife Conservation Commission held a press conference to discuss Crews' blood-alcohol level, which was above the legal limit. DiBiasio had to call Laurie Crews, and inform her that her husband was legally intoxicated while driving the boat and, subsequently, ramming it into the pier.

The Dodgers joined the Indians for a memorial service in a small auditorium in Winter Haven. Then, the front office had to decide how to move on. When could the team play? How quickly could the players regain focus? The regular season was less than two weeks away. Team president Hank Peters suggested the team return to action swiftly rather than sit around and sulk. Hargrove argued that they needed time to grieve. Peters countered that playing would be part of the grieving process.

"There's no handbook that teaches you," DiBiasio said.

They returned to the field a couple of days after the tragedy. On April 5, 1993, the last Opening Day at Cleveland Stadium, the Indians wore a patch on their jersey sleeves to commemorate their late teammates. The team presented jerseys, folded nice and neat, to Patti and Laurie in a pregame ceremony. The Yankees lined up along the third-base line. Every player and coach on the Indians' side had tears dripping from each eye.

Prior to first pitch, DiBiasio walked past the Yankees' dugout. There sat Wade Boggs, sobbing.

"I didn't know you and Steve were close," DiBiasio said.

"I didn't know him," Boggs replied. "But he's a brother."

8 Ring the Belle

The man with the muscle, the stout frame, and the surly scowl had plenty of nicknames. Some, he embraced. Others, no one said to his face.

Albert Belle, ever the explosive personality, has cultivated a tumultuous relationship with the Indians organization ever since he first donned a Tribe uniform in 1989. He was Joey. He was Albert. He was Mr. Freeze. He was Snapper. And through it all—through the corked bats, the bulging bicep, the spats with reporters, the run-ins and chase-downs with trick-or-treaters, the fits of rage in the clubhouse—he remained the same driven individual who simply wanted to be the best. He also wanted to be paid like the best.

"They put a thoroughbred in the gates to run the Kentucky Derby and they have the blinders on [him]," said Bob DiBiasio, Indians senior vice president of public affairs. "When he put his tunnel vision on, his blinders, to get ready to compete at a high level and you tried to penetrate those blinders on Albert, he bit your head off. You had to learn when you could connect with him."

Nearly two decades after Belle played his final game for the Indians, DiBiasio gave the former slugger a call. The two had maintained contact off and on since he departed the organization that drafted him in the second round out of LSU in 1987. DiBiasio asked Belle if he would grant his approval on the team creating a bobblehead in his likeness.

"It's about time!" Belle responded.

Before DiBiasio could utter another word, Belle requested that the ceramic model pose in the stance the once-chiseled outfielder made infamous. In Game 1 of the 1995 American League Division Series, after Belle's 11th-inning home run off of Red Sox reliever Rick Aguilera, Boston skipper Kevin Kennedy asked umpires to check the outfielder's bat for a cork filling. Though untimely, it wasn't the most far-fetched request. Belle had been caught red-handed a year earlier and slapped with a suspension. This time, though, it was all in the muscle. Belle stood on the edge of the dugout, demanded attention from the Red Sox bench and pointed to his flexed right bicep, which was bulging out from under his uniform sleeve, a patch of white cotton that appeared to be hanging on for dear life.

"Bobbleheads are no good unless they tell a real story," DiBiasio said.

Belle's story has many layers, many unforgettable incidents, and many learning experiences.

While at Triple A Colorado Springs in 1990, he destroyed a clubhouse sink during a fit of rage, which earned him a five-game suspension. Later that summer, he checked into counseling to cope with his alcohol dependency. After two months of help at the Cleveland Clinic, Belle issued a statement that declared he had received the necessary help and that he was now to be referred to by his first name, Albert. He had previously gone by the nickname Joey, short for Jojuan, his middle name.

No matter the moniker, the fiery personality remained the same. He was kicked out of the Puerto Rican winter league in 1990 for his typical temper tantrums. In May 1991, he pegged a heckling fan in the chest with a baseball. That merited him a six-game ban. A year later, he charged the mound after Kansas City hurler Neal Heaton heaved a pair of pitches that he deemed too close for comfort. Both players were ejected, as the benches cleared and players spilled out onto the field. Belle received a three-game suspension. In May 1993, Belle brawled with Royals pitcher Hipolito Pichardo after the right-hander plunked him in the shoulder. As a result, he was hit with another three-game ban.

In July 1994, White Sox manager Gene Lamont accused Belle of employing a corked bat. The lumber was confiscated and stored in the umpires' locker room to be examined. After the game, the umpires discovered the bat had been switched, so the Indians were required to hand over another one, which contained cork. Belle contended that the White Sox swiped his bat and corked it. Nonetheless, he was slapped with a seven-game suspension.

Reporters learned to stay out of Belle's way. He was known to gripe or yell if a member of the media looked at him in a certain manner or even said hello to him. Prior to Game 3 of the 1995 World Series, he shouted obscenities at reporters in the Indians dugout as they prepared to conduct interviews. Belle was later fined $50,000 for his actions.

His temper warranted him the nickname "Snapper" from some of his teammates. He could erupt, without warning, at any moment. He earned the nickname "Mr. Freeze" after he grumbled about the temperature in the clubhouse, turned down the thermostat and then shattered it with a bat. He once executed the same treatment on Kenny Lofton's boom box.

On Halloween in 1995, a group of teenagers tossed eggs at his house after he refused to supply them with candy. So, Belle chased after them in his SUV. He was convicted of reckless operation of a motor vehicle and fined for the incident. In 1996, Belle struck a photographer with a baseball and he knocked Milwaukee Brewers second baseman Fernando Vina to the ground with a sturdy forearm because Vina was standing in his path in the baseline as he

Do Not Pass Go

Upon his first visit to Cleveland after bolting for greener pastures following the 1996 campaign, Albert Belle was showered with colorful paper money from the board game Monopoly while he manned his position in left field.

"You smile at creativity," said Bob DiBiasio, Indians senior vice president of public affairs. "You can't avoid it. That's really about all you can say about that."

After a string of stat-stuffing seasons for the Indians, Belle joined the White Sox on a five-year, $55 million contract that made him the league's highest-paid player—a goal Belle had long maintained. Indians fans didn't take too kindly to the slugger's departure.

"I don't think it sat well with our fan base," DiBiasio said. "As long as it's only paper money on the field and nothing more significant, and people behave themselves—that's why you smile at the creativity end of it."

tried to turn a double play. Belle served a two-game suspension for his bullying of Vina.

"He wasn't easy," DiBiasio said.

For years, the Indians put up with his antics because of what he provided on the field. He recorded the first 50/50 season in major league history when he tallied 50 home runs and 52 doubles in only 143 games in 1995. He was named to four consecutive All-Star teams while with the Tribe. He led the American League in RBIs on three occasions. He finished in the top three in the balloting for the Most Valuable Player award each season from 1994–1996. During those years, he logged a .325 batting average, .414 on-base percentage, and .671 slugging percentage, averaging 42 doubles, 45 home runs, and 125 RBIs. All six of the walk-off home runs he swatted in his career came during that stretch. Two of them were grand slams.

"When I think of Albert," said team president Mark Shapiro, "I think of an intense competitor, a driven person, a meticulous work ethic. Mean. Just a tough guy. He was a reliable guy. He came to play every single day and then he was driven to put up and produce every day. You knew what you were going to get from Albert. This guy was going to be fueled to help us succeed and achieve his personal success. He was an incredibly productive and intimidating offensive performer."

Belle's peak production coincided with the team's ascent from a bottom-feeder to a perennial World Series contender. The team reached the Fall Classic in 1995 and qualified for the postseason in '96. And yet, it wasn't enough. The ego was always there, though not in a self-absorbed, pompous fashion. Belle simply presented an unfiltered, steadfast belief in his ability. He was dead set in his ways, unwavering in his conviction that his on-field exploits deserved proper compensation and acknowledgement. His personal goals received precedence. He strived to be the highest-paid player in the league, an aim that triggered the deterioration of his relationship with the Indians organization. He hit the free-agent market and the White Sox—Cleveland's AL Central adversary and the team that uncorked the secret behind his booming bats—scooped him up with a five-year, $55 million pact.

Tribe fans were upset by how the situation unfolded, how a player who served as part of a blossoming team could abandon everything for a self-fulfilling cause. That Belle acted in such a manner, however, surprised no one. Perhaps the vanquishing of his baggage and his inevitable tirades and tantrums and riots would cleanse the clubhouse. The team certainly had the lineup pieces to cope with his departure, especially since general manager John Hart swung a trade for powerful third baseman Matt Williams.

Belle proceeded to bat .274 with 30 home runs in his first season on the South Side. When he made his first appearance at Jacobs Field as the enemy on June 3, 1997, fans showered him with debris in left field. He resumed his offensive onslaught in 1998, when he compiled a .328 batting average, .399 on-base percentage, and .655 slugging percentage, with 49 home runs, 152 RBIs, and 48 doubles.

After the '98 campaign, he invoked a clause in his contract that required he remain one of the three highest-paid players in the league. Chicago refused to meet his contract demands, so he became a free agent and signed a five-year, $65 million deal with the Baltimore Orioles. Belle hit 60 home runs over two years for the O's before a degenerative hip condition forced him into retirement.

More than a decade passed. Belle and his wife started a family and he became a stay-at-home father to his four daughters. In late February 2012, Belle visited Indians spring training in Goodyear, Arizona. He reconnected with former teammates Lofton, Carlos Baerga and Sandy Alomar Jr., and his old manager Mike Hargrove. They reminisced and joked and laughed. Belle conversed with a handful of the active players.

Fences were mended. Relationships were reconciled. A year later, a reminder of the old Belle greeted fans at Progressive Field in the form of a bobblehead.

"Time has a way of calming things down," DiBiasio said.

9 Planning Ahead

In May 1990, voters passed a referendum that would tax sales of alcohol and cigarettes in Cuyahoga County. The money collected would finance a new ballpark for the Indians.

"I think if there were a club that people in baseball said needs to be moved in the late '80s and early '90s, it would have been the Indians," said former general manager John Hart. "Our owner made it very clear that wasn't going to happen. The politicians and the city made a decision to keep the club in Cleveland."

At that time, the Indians front office executives knew they would have a brand new, state of the art ballpark on the forefront of downtown in less than five years. They also knew they needed to field a team worthy of such an edifice. They could strike gold if they built a club that blossomed just as the new venue opened.

They did just that.

"Deep down, they were hoping beyond hope that we used it as a marketing tool, that as people saw this place sprouting from the ground, so was the team, and they'd intersect at the same time," said Bob DiBiasio, Indians senior vice president of public affairs. "When it was time to move in here, we'd have a team that would compete. That was definitely the hope."

The wheels started turning later in 1989. The Indians acquired 23-year-old Sandy Alomar Jr. and 21-year-old Carlos Baerga from the Padres for Joe Carter. The 29-year-old Carter had emerged as a force in the center of Cleveland's lineup, but by the time the Indians would be ready to contend, he would be past his prime. Two years later, the club acquired Kenny Lofton from Houston. Two years after that, Omar Vizquel relocated to Cleveland from Seattle.

When Gabe Paul ran the franchise in the '60s, he operated on the merits of showcasing star power to attract fans. He reacquired former fan favorite Rocky Colavito, who had been traded away years earlier. It did not work. The team struggled.

This was a different approach, one installed by Hank Peters and John Hart. The trades flooded the farm system with burgeoning talent. The club excelled in the amateur draft, as Albert Belle (1987, second round), Charles Nagy (1988, first round), Jim Thome (1989, 13th round), Manny Ramirez (1991, first round), and Chad Ogea (1991, third round) all eventually paid dividends.

Change in Ownership

Dick Jacobs and his brother, David, purchased the Indians in 1986. Steve O'Neill had owned the franchise until his death in 1983 and his estate owned the organization thereafter until the Jacobs got involved. Under Dick Jacobs' ownership—David died in 1992—the Indians enjoyed a resurgence following four decades of malaise.

In 2000, Larry Dolan bought the team for $323 million, more than eight times what Jacobs had paid for it 14 years earlier. Jacobs paid $6.3 million to keep the name of the ballpark as Jacobs Field for another six years. It was renamed Progressive Field in 2008.

Of course, the Indians had no idea that their tactic would actually pan out. They had accumulated a cluster of young talent, but they needed the kids to develop in time.

"You didn't know that Kenny Lofton, who couldn't hit out of a paper bag in the minor leagues, would turn into something special, which he ended up doing," DiBiasio said. "Or that Sandy and Carlos and Charlie, who you thought could perform, do end up performing. It was by design, but no one would have stood up and said, 'Yeah, we're going to make it happen,' because you just never know.

"But that was the goal. 'When we move into that place, let's have ourselves a team that's ready to truly compete for more than a year.'"

In between his tantrums and lack of hustle, Belle blossomed as a feared power hitter. He led the league with 129 RBIs in 1993. Nagy became an All-Star in his second full year in 1992. That same year, Lofton's first with the Tribe, the center fielder led the league in stolen bases and finished second in balloting for American League Rookie of the Year.

"We knew we had talent," Shapiro said. "Seeing Albert Belle start to emerge, seeing what Jim Thome was capable of. Sandy Alomar, Charlie Nagy, Carlos Baerga. There were certain guys that already started to demonstrate it. Other guys were clearly getting close."

Shapiro joined the organization as a baseball operations assistant in January 1992. He was hooked right away by Hart's conception.

"I bought into it," Shapiro said. "John was a pretty persuasive guy with a strong vision and one he was passionate about. The vision that they painted and the plan that they talked about was, 'We have a core of young players and we are going to be developing and peaking as a team coinciding with moving into a new ballpark, and that will allow us the revenues to be able to keep the team together.' It was that simple."

The next step of the plan included the team locking up some of its rising stars, such as Alomar and Baerga, to long-term, affordable contracts.

"We tied these guys up to multi-year deals, getting control of free-agent years and arbitration years and a lot of cost-certainty for long-term deals," Shapiro said. "We did that on a mass scale, with some guys who ended up being core players and some guys who didn't."

In 1993, the Indians amassed a 76–86 record for the second straight year. They were better, though. They scored more runs (790 to 674) and improved their run differential by 50 runs. Their starting rotation was a train wreck, but their core pieces had developed as hoped. The team was clearly on the ascent and was prepared to move into its new building, so it complemented its talented youth with established veterans. On December 2, 1993, the Indians introduced Dennis Martinez and Eddie Murray as free-agent acquisitions at the new ballpark. There was a shift in perception about the club. Fans finally had a reason to back their team and opposing players had justification for respecting it.

By the time Opening Day on April 4, 1994, arrived, there was a palpable energy and buzz about the team, its new home, and its future. The blueprint sketched out five years earlier had worked. Now it was all about converting it into a period of sustainable success.

"It's rare that a plan that's articulated like that comes to be like that one did," Shapiro said. "There were probably things involved in that that weren't part of the plan, like the Browns not being here, which was part of it extending and being as successful as it was. It was just a magical time."

10 Ten Cent Beer Night

The crude chants and obscene shouts? Those were one thing. The streakers and flashers were another. The trespassers and the arrests were a different story. The disruption of a major league game was the final straw.

So much went wrong at Cleveland Stadium on June 4, 1974, that the night lives on in sports infamy. Certainly, had the Indians—and, more specifically, Jackie York and Carl Fazio, the organization's promotions team—had any inkling that the night may have gone awry, they would have scrapped the idea. But in 1971, they held Nickel Beer Night. It went on without a hitch.

"It went smoothly," said Bob DiBiasio, Indians senior vice president for public affairs. "They thought they'd do it again and raise it to a dime. But there were issues."

A week earlier, the Indians played at Arlington Stadium in Texas, where the Rangers hosted their own Ten Cent Beer Night. After a bench-clearing brawl, fans became unruly and heaved beer and food at Cleveland's players in the visitors' dugout. Rangers manager Billy Martin did not endear himself to the Cleveland

Fans became increasingly rowdy on Ten Cent Beer Night at Cleveland Stadium on June 4, 1974. Their belligerence intensified from standing atop the dugouts to finally storming the field in the ninth inning.

community when he claimed the city lacked the number of fans necessary to repeat those actions when the teams met again a week later.

"They won't have enough fans to worry about," Martin quipped.

Martin taunted the fans at Cleveland Stadium by blowing them a kiss prior to first pitch on June 4. That did not help measures, either.

Cleveland radio host Pete Franklin doused the fire with gasoline when he spent the days leading up to the Rangers' arrival by building up the rivalry, Martin's antics, and the need for retaliation. He urged fans to venture to the ballpark.

"A lot of people think Pete Franklin had something to do with it," DiBiasio said. "When we were in fisticuffs with the Rangers on the previous road trip and the radio was playing up that fireworks were going to be happening at the game—you add the beer to it..."

The cheap beer—a drink that typically cost about 65 cents at the time—provided the final spark for the crowd of 25,134. Throughout the game, fans were removing clothes, running onto the field, throwing hot dogs, and yelling obscenities. One woman bolted onto the field in an attempt to kiss umpire Nestor Chylak. Fans tried to slide into bases. They pulled down their pants and mooned the crowd. A man wearing nothing but one black sock streaked across the field.

In the ninth inning, everything took a turn for the worse. The Indians had tied the game, 5–5, with a pair of runs in the final frame. Then, one fan entered the field of play in an attempt to retrieve the hat off of the head of Rangers right fielder Jeff Burroughs. He ran up behind Burroughs, snatched the ball cap, dropped it, looked up and locked eyes with the player. Burroughs attempted to kick the fan and fell down and fans spilled out onto the field and swarmed Burroughs. A melee broke out. Rangers players poured out of the dugout, wielding bats, in support of Burroughs. The Indians followed suit, joining forces with their American League adversaries to fend off the feisty fans. Tribe reliever Tom Hilgendorf was struck in the head with a steel folding chair. It was pure, belligerent, hops-infused chaos. Fans stole all three bases on the infield.

The umpires called the game. The Indians were forced to forfeit. Some left the field bearing wounds. Some were taken to the hospital. Some were arrested. The Indians never held Ten Cent Beer Night again...until July 18, a mere 45 days later. That night, they limited fans to two beers per transaction.

11 Hometown Hero

Sandy Alomar Jr.'s 1997 season was nothing short of magical. Had it been a Hollywood script, it would have been deemed too cheesy and unrealistic to excel at the box office.

The veteran catcher socked a home run in five consecutive games during the season's first week. After the Indians' first seven games—he played in six of them—he was batting .538 with five home runs, 13 RBIs, and a 1.231 slugging percentage. He had multi-hit games in seven of his first eight contests and 21 hits overall. On April 13, he was batting .618. That was just a precursor of how the rest of his campaign would unfold.

Alomar had come back to Earth once the weather warmed up. He entered a game against the Orioles on May 25 with a .331 average. He went 1-for-4 in that affair. He followed that up with two hits the next day in Chicago and one base knock the day after that. This became a pattern. Alomar strung together a 30-game hitting streak before he finally went hitless in an 0-for-4 effort in Minnesota on July 10, the Indians' first game following the All-Star break.

In Cleveland's 8–2 loss to Minnesota at the Metrodome, Alomar struck out in the second and fourth innings, grounded out in the seventh, and popped out for the final out in the ninth. He fell one game short of the franchise-record hitting streak of 31 games, logged by Nap Lajoie in 1906. He fell four games short of Benito Santiago's record mark for a catcher, established in 1987, Santiago's rookie campaign.

It wasn't as though Alomar cooled off during the All-Star break. He tallied a crucial hit in the Midsummer Classic, too. In the eighth inning of the annual duel between the American and

National leagues, Alomar slugged a 2–2 off-speed pitch from San Francisco's Shawn Estes into the left-field bleachers for a go-ahead two-run home run. The long ball broke a 1–1 tie with two outs in the seventh inning.

Joe Buck's call to a national TV audience declared Alomar a "hometown hero," as the catcher sent those in attendance into a frenzy. The American League held on for a 3–1 victory. Alomar became the first player to club a home run in the All-Star Game in his home ballpark since Braves slugger Hank Aaron teed off at Atlanta Stadium in 1972.

Alomar dedicated the game to his grandmother, who had passed away four days earlier. He earned the Most Valuable Player award, which he lifted high in one hand while he held his son, Marcus, in the other. Alomar attributed his performance—both during the game and overall that season—to his good health. Injuries limited Alomar to fewer than 90 games in each season from 1991–1995.

Alomar finished the regular season with a .324 batting average, .545 slugging percentage, 21 home runs, 83 RBIs, and 37 doubles, all career-best marks. He racked up 15 hits that gave the Indians the lead in a game. He batted .321 with runners in scoring position and .309 with runners in scoring position and two outs. He hit .397 with a 1.043 OPS when the game was considered "late and close" and .371 with a 1.024 OPS during "high leverage" situations.

No at-bat came with more on the line than his trip to the plate in the eighth inning of Game 4 of the American League Division Series against the New York Yankees. Four outs from elimination, the Indians trailed 2–1 in the game and 2–1 in the series. With two outs and no runners on in the eighth, Alomar sent a 2-0 pitch from 27-year-old, first-time All-Star reliever Mariano Rivera into the first row of seats in right field. The game-tying home run saved the Indians' season. Alomar shouted, wound up his right arm and pumped his fist as the ball landed out of the reach of Yankees right fielder Paul O'Neill.

"I cherish that postseason," Alomar said, "and hitting the home run against Mariano was huge because it gave us a chance to go to the next game, in which we ended up beating the Yankees. That, to me, is what baseball is all about. It's about winning games and championships. That was the most important home run in my career."

Omar Vizquel delivered an RBI single in the ninth to force a decisive Game 5. Once Brian Giles squeezed the baseball in his glove on Bernie Williams' fly out to left field, Cleveland claimed that contest, 4–3, to advance to the American League Championship Series against the Baltimore Orioles. Alomar's home run the previous night, though, is remembered for rescuing an eventual World Series team from an early postseason dismissal.

How many players can boast about a clutch home run in both the Midsummer Classic and the postseason? Alomar understandably covets the October long ball a bit more.

"That was more fun, when we were playing the Yankees in the postseason and had the chance to beat them," Alomar said. "Hitting home runs in the postseason are more challenging and important than a home run in the All-Star Game."

Bob DiBiasio, the Indians' senior vice president of public affairs, recalls the sellout crowd of 45,231 remaining in Jacobs Field long after the final pitch of Game 4 of the American League Division Series. He can remember hearing car horns in downtown Cleveland two hours after the game ended.

"It was the loudest thing I have ever heard in my life," DiBiasio said. "People didn't want to leave. We had a game to play the next day, but people didn't want to leave the ballpark. They all huddled around. It was one of the most incredible nights."

It was a microcosm of Alomar's miraculous 1997 season.

"For the first time, I felt completely healthy," Alomar said. "I had so many problems with the microfracture [surgery] that I had, that I had to make a lot of adjustments in my mechanics and stuff like that. That year, I felt like I put it together. I felt pretty good. It was a fun year. But more importantly, I was able to help the team and we were able to go to the World Series. That was the most fun year I had."

12 Check out Heritage Park

Beyond the center-field fence at Progressive Field, tucked behind the trees and shrubs that give the concourse a green thumb, in a space previously occupied by picnic tables, resides a shrine of Indians lore.

It is hallowed ground, filled with beacons of history. It is a refreshing spot to visit before or during a game, a place to learn, to reminisce, to appreciate. It is dubbed Heritage Park and it was unveiled on Opening Day in 2007 as a means "to preserve Indians history," "to honor excellence," and "to connect generations," as detailed on a plaque at the center's entrance.

Walk down a short set of steps to the area's rotunda, where all members of the franchise's Hall of Fame have a plaque with a depiction of them. There is Sandy Alomar Jr. in full catcher's gear, with his mask resting on the top of his head. There is Rocky Colavito, holding his bat high above his head with both arms. There is Bob Feller, rocking back into his patented windup, with his left leg stretched out into the air. There is Mike Hargrove, the "Human Rain Delay," doing what he did best: stepping out of the batter's box with one foot and regrouping in a means of stalling for

Top Achievements

There are 34 large, dark bricks in Heritage Park that commemorate some of the franchise's most prolific individual achievements. Here is a complete list.

- Gaylord Perry won the American League Cy Young award in 1972
- Sam McDowell tossed back-to-back one-hit shutouts in 1966
- Albert Belle became the first player in franchise history to hit 50 home runs in a season in 1995
- Chris James set a club record with nine RBIs in a game on May 4, 1991 (and Lonnie Chisenhall tied it in June 2014)
- Dick Bosman threw a no-hitter against the defending champion Oakland Athletics on July 19, 1974
- Rocky Colavito slugged four home runs in one game on June 10, 1959
- Herb Score was named American League Rookie of the Year in 1955
- Len Barker threw a perfect game on May 15, 1981
- Al Rosen clubbed two home runs during the 1954 All-Star Game
- "Shoeless" Joe Jackson batted .408 in 1911
- Jolbert Cabrera slapped the game-winning single in the Indians' 15–14 win against the Mariners on August 15, 2001
- Sandy Alomar Jr. was named the 1997 All-Star Game Most Valuable Player
- The Indians hit four consecutive home runs during a win against the Los Angeles Angels on July 31, 1963
- Marquis Grissom stole home for the winning run in Game 3 of the 1997 American League Championship Series against the Baltimore Orioles
- The Indians sold out 455 straight games from 1995–2001
- Tony Fernandez socked the game-winning home run in Game 6 of the 1997 American League Championship Series
- Dennis Eckersley strung together $22\frac{1}{3}$ consecutive hitless innings in 1977
- CC Sabathia hurled his first big league shutout on August 15, 2003
- Travis Hafner hit six grand slams in 2006
- Kevin Kouzmanoff slugged a grand slam on the first pitch he saw in his major league career on September 2, 2006
- Bob Feller won the pitching triple crown in 1940

- Frank Robinson became baseball's first African American manager in 1975
- Earl Averill hit a home run in his first major league at-bat in 1929
- Johnny Burnett set a big league record with nine hits in a game on July 10, 1932
- The Indians registered their first win in the American League on April 27, 1901
- Bob Feller recorded 17 strikeouts in a game as a rookie on September 13, 1936
- Lou Boudreau went 4-for-4 in a one-game playoff against the Boston Red Sox in 1948 to determine the American League World Series representative
- Larry Doby broke the American League color barrier with the Indians in 1947
- Bob Feller threw the sport's only Opening Day no-hitter in 1940
- Luis Tiant tossed four straight shutouts in 1968
- Addie Joss threw the franchise's first perfect game in 1908
- The Indians recorded the first postseason unassisted triple play and grand slam in Game 5 of the 1920 World Series
- Kenny Lofton won the American League stolen base crown for five consecutive years from 1992-96
- Stan Coveleski earned three victories during the 1920 World Series

time. There is Kenny Lofton, his eyes glued to the pitcher, with his hands gripping a bat as he prepares to lay down a bunt. There is Omar Vizquel, his left knee gracing the infield dirt, making a back-handed stop from his shortstop position. There are Larry Doby and Carlos Baerga, clutching their bats with their right hands after following through on a swing.

The ground is made up of bricks that bear names of—and messages from—fans. Each section of bricks is topped with a dark gray square dedicated to a specific achievement. There is a square commemorating Frank Robinson for becoming the first African American manager in major league history. There is a square honoring Addie Joss for throwing the franchise's first perfect game.

There is a square noting Kenny Lofton's five consecutive American League stolen base titles.

Take another set of steps down to a vast, open area, where on a giant brick wall rest squares with the names and signatures of the top 100 all-time players in franchise history and the 100th anniversary starting lineup, chosen by fans in 2001. Fans can read about Cleveland's Negro League history (the Cleveland Buckeyes played in the league from 1943–1948 and again briefly in 1950) or about the sad tale of Ray Chapman, who is honored with a large plaque and a script about his story. There is a plaque to honor Doby and two smaller displays with information about Steve Olin and Tim Crews, a pair of Tribe relievers who died in a boating accident during spring training in 1993. An oversized bronze baseball that bears the club's "Distinguished Hall of Fame" for non-uniformed personnel is also on display. That includes past owners Bill Veeck and Dick Jacobs; broadcasters Mike Hegan, Jimmy Dudley, and Jack Graney; front office executives John Hart and Cy Slapnicka; and athletic trainer Jimmy Warfield.

Heritage Park serves as a mecca of Indians history, a destination spot for anyone fascinated by the greatest feats and figures in the franchise's existence.

13 Little O

About halfway along his two-and-a-half-hour trek to Cleveland from Detroit, Omar Vizquel exited the turnpike near Sandusky, Ohio, to grab something to drink. He was en route to his old stomping grounds, Progressive Field, to coach first base for the Tigers and be inducted into the Indians Hall of Fame.

When he pulled up to the tollbooth, the employee recognized Vizquel and "went crazy." She pleaded with him to get out of his car and take a picture with her.

"It was something that I couldn't believe," Vizquel said. "The whole World Series thing and the whole Cleveland era was in the 1990s. We had some great teams and here we are [20 years later] and people still remember the name, remember the face."

Who could have projected that when Vizquel opted to embark on a career in baseball?

Anyone who watched a teenage Omar Vizquel play in winter ball in Venezuela in the 1980s came away with two conclusions: the diminutive shortstop couldn't hit the ball out of the infield, but he also didn't even need a glove to field his position.

It takes a diverse skill set to last 24 years in the major leagues. Vizquel compensated for his deficiencies. To mask his pedestrian arm strength, he perfected the art of proper positioning, which reduced the number of daunting heaves he had to make from deep in the hole.

The kid who couldn't hit a lick racked up 2,877 career hits, four more than Babe Ruth. Following the suggestion made by Bill Plummer, his winter ball manager and coach with the Mariners, Vizquel learned to switch-hit. Shifting to the left-handed side of the batter's box provided him with a shorter path to first base to beat out bunts and infield hits.

"He made himself into a good hitter," Plummer said. "He worked hard at it."

Vizquel batted .230 over his first three major league seasons with the Mariners. He often doubted his ability and how long he would last at the big league level with such an unreliable piece of lumber. His defense, however, kept him afloat.

"He amazed you each day when you watch him day in and day out," Plummer said. "You expect him to make every play, which he did."

Plummer became Seattle's skipper in 1992. He batted Vizquel leadoff the majority of his time in Seattle, sometimes plugging him into the No. 2 spot in his lineup. Vizquel proceeded to bat .294 in 1992. The following season, he received his first of 11 Gold Glove awards. After the 1993 campaign, however, the Mariners traded him to Cleveland for Felix Fermin and Reggie Jefferson. Vizquel's

Speed Racer

Sandy Alomar Jr. likes to reflect upon the day he was coasting along the highway, heading to the ballpark, when he peered into his rearview mirror and saw a "screaming yellow Porsche convertible" chasing him down.

"He was trying to catch me and blow my doors away," Alomar said.

It was Omar Vizquel, in his infamous vehicle, which he had custom-made in Germany. When they arrived at Jacobs Field, the two laughed about their high-speed highway pursuit.

The Indians inducted Vizquel into their Hall of Fame on June 21, 2014. Vizquel left his newly unveiled plaque in Heritage Park, beyond the center-field fence, and jogged in from the bullpen to a podium set up at the pitcher's mound. As he crossed into the infield, Carlos Baerga flipped him a baseball. Vizquel made a leaping, bare-handed catch, reminiscent of hundreds he made during his career as a perennial Gold Glove Award-winning shortstop.

Vizquel delivered a speech to a sold-out crowd and then took a lap around the field as a passenger in a yellow Porsche convertible, modeled after the one he drove around town during his 11 years in Cleveland. The trip around the field might have marked the only time Vizquel's Porsche ever adhered to the speed limit.

Vizquel always found ways to have fun. Any time the team had a day off, he and Baerga went to a museum, the beach, or a concert. They played percussion with bands and went to clubs.

"His energy was infectious every day," said pitcher Charles Nagy, "running around with a smile on his face, just enjoying baseball and enjoying life."

then-wife, a Seattle native, cried when she learned of the deal. The couple had just purchased a house in the area.

Vizquel's career, though, took off in Cleveland, where he began to bat second regularly. The trade proved to be a heist for the Tribe. Fermin played in only 185 games the rest of his career. Jefferson played in 512, but only 63 with the Mariners. Vizquel played in 1,478 games with the Indians and lasted for another eight years after his tenure beside Lake Erie. He earned his way onto three American League All-Star teams, played on six Cleveland postseason squads and developed a reputation as the game's premier defender. He submitted dazzling displays with his bare hands. He dirtied his jersey by making diving stops. He turned his back toward home plate to catch pop-ups while fighting the high, bright sun.

"The thing that I'll always remember is it would be 100 degrees out there, the sun is so bright," said his former teammate Kenny Lofton. "We all need our shades on to catch a fly ball. But Omar is the only guy on the field with no shades on. I'm trying to figure out what the heck he's doing. All of a sudden, a fly ball hits and we look and say, 'What is Omar going to do?' He's the only guy I know who turns his back to the hitter and catches the fly ball over his shoulder. I'm still amazed by that. It's something that I tell people about all the time, to look at tape of Omar doing that.

Plummer said he made it look like he "never got a bad hop." Sandy Alomar Jr. marveled at Vizquel's acrobatic flair, his instincts and his throwing accuracy.

"How many times did you turn the TV on and see Omar making a play that made you gasp?" said Indians manager Terry Francona. "He was pretty incredible."

The Indians made Vizquel the 40th inductee into their team Hall of Fame in June 2014. His credentials could warrant him a place in Cooperstown as well.

Vizquel ranks among the top 10 in franchise history in games played, runs scored, hits, doubles, walks, and stolen bases. And then, of course, there's his defense.

"You kept thinking he was going to get eaten up by a ball, but he never did," Plummer said. "He made some great plays. You just can't teach it."

14 Swing and a Drive

Maybe.

It's a word with which Herb Score qualified his historic call, a five-letter filler that hedged the radio announcer's premature exclamation.

"The Indians are going back to the World Series!" Score shouted once Tony Fernandez's fly ball landed in the first row of seats atop the right-field wall at Oriole Park at Camden Yards.

"Maybe," he then added, realizing that Baltimore still had its last at-bat in the bottom half of the 11th inning.

It was the perfect, memorable, flawed moment to cap a wacky, dramatic, mistake-filled set of six games. Fernandez wasn't even supposed to play that day. Bip Roberts was drilled on the left thumb by a line drive during batting practice. He was unable to properly grip a bat, which made him unavailable for Game 6. Naturally, Fernandez was the culprit at the plate who unintentionally injured his fellow second baseman.

The injury to Roberts—the team's leadoff hitter and spark plug, acquired from Kansas City on August 31 of that year—left the Tribe brass bummed out. Fernandez, a defensive specialist who had a surprisingly sufficient season at the plate—a .286 average with 11 home runs—would get the nod instead. Vice president of public relations Bob DiBiasio approached general manager John Hart and said: "John, this is how stories are made. He wasn't supposed to play, so he's going to win the game for us."

Cleveland's Charles Nagy and Baltimore's Mike Mussina dueled for eight innings, albeit in different styles. Nagy scattered nine hits and three walks over 7⅓ frames. He bent, but did not break. He allowed at least one base runner in all but one inning he pitched, but he managed to escape unharmed each time.

"Charlie was on edge every inning," DiBiasio said. "They had guys on base every inning and he got out of it every inning."

Mussina was dominant. He submitted a dazzling effort in Game 3 of the series four days earlier, when he logged a League Championship Series record 15 strikeouts over seven innings. In Game 6, he permitted only one hit—a David Justice leadoff double in the fifth—and issued only two free passes, while tallying 10 strikeouts. The scoreless tie persisted until the 11th inning, when Fernandez tagged Armando Benitez with two outs.

The Indians had Benitez solved that series. They knew that when he held his glove a certain way once he set on the mound, he would deliver a particular pitch. Fernandez waved his bat behind his head as he stood in his slightly opened stance. As Benitez reared back, Fernandez—sporting calf-high blue socks to accent his gray uniform—rocked back and executed his high leg kick. He offered a smooth stroke at a hanging slider over the heart of the plate. Right fielder Jerome Walton watched the baseball sail into the front row of fans perched atop the tall fence. The Indians' dugout erupted.

Fernandez had made an oracle out of both Score and DiBiasio. The Indians were off to the World Series.

Said DiBiasio: "John [Hart], in an ESPN interview after the game, said: 'Our PR guy told me he would do this.'"

15 Breaking Barriers

There was Neil Armstrong and there was Buzz Aldrin. There was Jackie Robinson and there was Larry Doby. Armstrong's presence on the moon did not make Aldrin's trip there any less demanding. Robinson's presence did not make Doby any less of a pioneer.

Robinson broke the Major League Baseball color barrier for the Brooklyn Dodgers at the start of the 1947 season. It was a calculated operation and both Robinson and the Dodgers had time to prepare. Doby's addition to the Indians was done more hastily and was kept from public knowledge. Like Robinson, he dealt with cold shoulders from teammates and backlash from opposing players and fans. Doby became the first African American player in the American League when he suited up for the Indians on July 5, 1947, at Comiskey Park in Chicago.

Doby had played mostly middle infield in the Negro Leagues, but Lou Boudreau and Joe Gordon were entrenched at shortstop and second base, respectively. So in his first big league season, Doby played sparingly, occasionally serving as a pinch-hitter. He blossomed during his first full season in 1948, as he posted a .301 batting average and .384 on-base percentage, with 14 home runs and 66 RBIs. He played center and right field and helped the Tribe to the American League pennant. The club defeated the Boston Braves in six games to capture its first World Series title in 28 years, and Doby became the first African American player to homer in a World Series game.

Doby developed into a middle-of-the-order threat and a perennial All-Star. He was selected to seven consecutive All-Star teams from 1949 –1955 and he slugged 20 or more home runs for eight straight seasons. Doby finished second in balloting for American

League Most Valuable Player in 1954, when he tied a career high with 32 home runs and established a personal best with 126 RBIs. That year, the Tribe tallied 111 wins in the regular season to put a temporary end to the New York Yankees' dominance. The New York Giants swept the Indians in the Fall Classic.

"To have Larry Doby as the first African American in the American League—life isn't wrapped in a nice, neat little bow and this is a perfect example," said Bob DiBiasio, Indians senior vice president of public affairs.

About seven years after he played his final big league game, Doby was elected into the Indians Hall of Fame in 1966. The team retired his No. 14 on July 3, 1994, and the Veteran's Committee inducted him into the Baseball Hall of Fame in 1998. On July 5, 2012, 65 years to the day he debuted with the Indians, the team renamed a portion of Eagle Avenue—the street that runs adjacent to the ballpark beyond left field—Larry Doby Way. When the Indians announced their intentions in 2014 to renovate Progressive Field, they revealed plans to construct a statue of Doby.

"Larry Doby did some historic things in this uniform," team president Mark Shapiro said.

16 A Bug's Life

Squirrels, seagulls, and chickens have played a hand in happenings at Progressive Field. No creature, however, can compare to the impact provided by swarms of midges in October 2007.

Just ask Joba Chamberlain.

In Game 2 of the 2007 American League Division Series between the Indians and Yankees, pesky bugs pushed the Tribe to victory and a 2–0 series lead. The infestation of little flies didn't seem to fluster Fausto Carmona, who tossed nine dazzling innings for the Indians. The right-hander limited New York to one run on three hits. Unfortunately for the Indians, Andy Pettitte matched him.

The Yankees carried a 1–0 lead into the eighth inning. Then, the midges stole the show. Chamberlain, clearly bothered by their presence, walked Grady Sizemore to start the eighth. He heaved a wild pitch, sending Sizemore to second. Asdrubal Cabrera bunted Sizemore to third. Travis Hafner lined out, but with Victor Martinez at the plate, Chamberlain tossed another wild pitch. Sizemore raced home from third to tie the game.

During the inning, Yankees staff attended to Chamberlain on the mound, as they sprayed down his uniform with insect repellant. Home-plate umpire Laz Diaz doused his body in the spray as well. He then passed the green can to Yankees shortstop Derek Jeter, who applied the stuff to his gray uniform. The rest of New York's infield joined in, as Alex Rodriguez and Robinson Cano covered their jerseys with the sticky substance.

The bugs latched onto Chamberlain's face and neck. The infielders spent the inning swatting them away, wiping them off, and trying to gain a line of sight toward the plate.

"I've never seen anything like that before," Jeter recalled seven years later, upon his final visit to Progressive Field as a player. "It was like that for both teams. It wasn't like they just came out when we decided to go on defense. Those were by far the oddest conditions I've played in. I didn't enjoy it. It wasn't fun. They were all over the place. You really couldn't shake them. That's what made it difficult."

There have been other odd conditions. The Indians defeated the Kansas City Royals 4–3 in 10 innings on June 11, 2009, when Shin-Soo Choo singled home the winning run. Choo chopped the base hit up the middle. A flock of seagulls had gathered in center field. When the baseball came bouncing in their direction, they scattered, shielding center fielder Coco Crisp's view. The ball deflected off the wing of one of the birds and rolled past Crisp as he attempted to corral it and fire a throw toward home plate. Instead, Mark Derosa scored and the Indians won.

Maybe it's just a dose of home-field advantage. The midges didn't appear to torment the Tribe the way they did the Yankees. Or was it simply a showcase of the Tribe's toughness?

"Both teams had the bugs," said team president Mark Shapiro, then the club's general manager. "It bothered one team. It didn't bother the other team. It wasn't like the bugs were only there for the Yankees. They were there for our guys, too.

"Fausto Carmona sat there and was so focused. There were bugs crawling all over his face and he didn't even notice it, whereas

What's My Age Again?

During the winter of 2012, the Indians learned that the 28-year-old Fausto Carmona was actually a 31-year-old hurler named Roberto Hernandez. The right-hander was arrested in his native Dominican Republic on charges of using a false name. He received a three-week suspension from Major League Baseball, restructured his contract with the Indians, and was required to perform community service.

Hernandez expressed remorse over his transgressions—he had assumed the identity of a distant cousin in order to convince the Indians he was 17 when they signed him in 2000. He did not, however, delve into the details of his ordeal.

His teammates didn't bother asking the tough questions. (Justin Masterson asked Hernandez if he could call him "Bob." Hernandez approved.) They took it easy on the pitcher. For the most part, at least.

Once Hernandez was granted a new visa and arrived at the Indians' clubhouse on July 22, 2012, his teammates presented him with three birthday cakes to cover the difference in his actual age. On a table sat one round cake with candles shaped in the numerals 2 and 9, as well as two rectangular-shaped cakes with plastic balloons and red, yellow, and green frosting.

A member of the Yankees staff sprays pitcher Joba Chamberlain with insect repellant late in Game 2 of the 2007 ALDS against the Indians. The bugs caused Chamberlain to give up the Yankees' lead in the eighth inning and seemingly helped the Indians, who weren't nearly as bothered by them, win the game.

Joba Chamberlain was spraying himself and swatting himself. There was Fausto, just locked in.

"I felt like that was a triumph of our toughness and our resilience. That's what stood out to me with that group of guys."

The game lasted until the 11th inning, when Hafner supplied a walk-off single with the bases loaded and two outs. Cleveland captured the series in four games and advanced to the American League Championship Series against the Red Sox.

Just how bedeviling were the bugs?

"I'm sure they'll be back," Jeter surmised. "Next time they're out, just stand outside for a little while. You'll be able to answer that."

17 Perfection

The game-time temperature was a chilly 49 degrees. Nearly 7,300 fans trickled into Cleveland Municipal Stadium. (Tens of thousands more claim to have been in attendance.) Len Barker never shies away from discussing the details of his pitching performance on May 15, 1981, when he tossed the 10th perfect game in major league history.

He remembers how much bite his curveball had that night. He started to throw the pitch with frequency after the third inning, even though he was more known for his heater. He remembers having pinpoint control. He could throw any pitch to any desired location and he would record a strike. He threw only 19 of his 103 pitches out of the zone. He remembers walking out to the mound for the ninth inning, how he picked the baseball up off the dirt, stepped on the rubber, dropped the ball and nearly fell off the mound because he was so nervous. Every time he is asked about that brisk, damp Friday night, he stresses that the historical feat was a team and city-wide achievement, not just an individual accolade.

Barker was in control from the start. He induced three quick groundouts in the first inning. He did not reach a three-ball count on any of the 27 batters he faced. On the Indians' radio broadcast, Herb Score noted: "You talk about having command of all your pitches. Len Barker has had that tonight."

The ninth inning arrived with the Indians ahead 3–0. A horde of reporters and cameramen gathered next to the dugout, ready to pounce. Rick Bosetti led off the frame for the Toronto Blue Jays and lifted a harmless pop fly into foul territory, short of third base. Toby Harrah squeezed it for the first out. Barker then fanned Al Woods on an off-speed pitch. Ernie Whitt, a pinch-hitter, was Toronto's last chance.

"Fly ball, center field," Score shouted as Whitt lofted Barker's offering to the outfield.

Center fielder Rick Manning spread his arms as wide as they could go to call off his fellow outfielders. He took a series of excited steps toward the spot where he would make the catch.

"Manning coming on. He's there."

In one, swift motion, Manning caught the ball, raised his arms above his head, jumped up and down and then sprinted in toward the mound.

"He catches it! Len Barker has pitched a no-hitter! A perfect game for Len Barker!"

Barker was immediately mobbed by catcher Ron Hassey and first baseman Mike Hargrove. Pitchers and media members followed. Barker had thrown the second perfect game in franchise history and the first in 73 years.

"It was exciting," Barker said, "not only for me and my teammates, but for the whole city of Cleveland."

Manning presented to Barker the baseball from the final out, but the hurler gave it right back to the center fielder.

"He came running in," Barker said, "gave me a hug and he asked me, he said: 'Here's the ball,' and I said, 'No. I'm giving it to you for all the things you've done.'

"It wasn't me just pitching a perfect game. It was the whole team and the whole city. That's the way I always treated it through my whole career. People would ask me and I'd say, 'No. It was all of us.'

"I couldn't have done it without my teammates and the city. They were always behind us."

18 The Clock Strikes 2:00 AM

Bob Costas and Bob Uecker had engaged in meaningless drivel. Only caffeine and a lack of a finite outcome were keeping them going.

Rick Manning and Bob DiBiasio were poking around the Indians clubhouse, looking for hot tea or Pepsi, anything they could find that would provide an energy boost. DiBiasio didn't drink coffee. Suddenly, a horde of players stampeded into the area as they continued the celebration they had commenced on the field.

Shortly after 2 AM on October 4, 1995, Cleveland had captured its first postseason victory in 47 years. Perhaps the most unlikely hero sent a full house of fading fans home happy.

The Indians were no strangers to dramatic victories at Jacobs Field in 1995. Among their 100 wins, 27 came in their final at-bat, including nine in the form of a home run. Albert Belle slugged three, Manny Ramirez clubbed two, and Sandy Alomar Jr., Jim

Thome, Paul Sorrento and Eddie Murray each delivered one. Tony Pena wasn't an offensive threat. He batted .262 with five home runs and 28 RBIs in 91 games for the Tribe in 1995. His role was to form a rapport with the pitching staff; hitting was secondary.

A 39-minute rain delay pushed back the game's first pitch. A 23-minute rain delay interrupted the eighth inning, with the score tied 3–3. Boston's Tim Naehring provided the Red Sox with a one-run advantage in the top of the 11th when he deposited a pitch from Jim Poole over the fence in left field. Belle, however, evened the score in the bottom of the frame as he swatted a Rick Aguilera offering into the bleachers. A third delay ensued when Boston manager Kevin Kennedy yelled to the umpires to confiscate Belle's bat, which the skipper contended was corked. Belle stared at the Red Sox from the home dugout, flexed his right bicep and pointed to the bulging muscle. The umpires checked the slugger's lumber, but found nothing afoul.

A Bulging Bicep

The pose is iconic in Cleveland, and not just because its likeness now exists as a bobblehead. After Albert Belle tied the score in Game 1 of the 1995 American League Division Series with a home run, Red Sox skipper Kevin Kennedy requested that the slugger's bat be checked for cork.

At that moment, Belle pointed to his right bicep and pointed to Indians history. That stance, from the Tribe dugout, would never be forgotten. As he flexed his muscle, veins protruded from his right forearm. His eyebrows curled as he initiated a menacing glare toward Boston's dugout. His mustache wrapped around his upper lip as he shouted at Kennedy. He squeezed his right fist as his bicep pushed his white uniform to its limit.

He seemed primed for a fistfight, ready for confrontation. His bat checked out clean. The Indians knocked out the Red Sox in three games to advance to the American League Championship Series against the Seattle Mariners.

When Pena stepped into the batter's box with two outs in the bottom of the 13th, the clock had ticked past 2 AM and Costas was taking playful jabs at Uecker's unheralded playing career. Red Sox southpaw reliever Zane Smith misfired with his first three offerings to the 38-year-old. Manager Mike Hargrove gave Pena the take sign. There was no need to swing at a 3-0 pitch, especially given Pena's offensive limitations. Pena didn't listen.

Uecker was mid-sentence when Costas cut him off and shrieked: "Oh man! Oh man! Tony Pena! On 3-and-0! Sends everybody home!"

Smith left a pitch over the plate. Pena took a healthy swing and immediately flipped his bat away, toward the Indians' dugout. The baseball landed in the first row of the bleachers, perched above the 19-foot-high wall in left field. A group of fans clad in orange ponchos chased after the ball as Pena raised both arms in the air and circled the bases. He slapped hands with second baseman Carlos Baerga before he was mobbed by the rest of his teammates at home plate.

The Indians hadn't competed in a playoff game since 1954, when they were swept in the World Series by the New York Giants. What a way to make the wait worthwhile. A wet, dreary night—turned morning—ended in thrilling fashion, a style to which Indians fans had quickly grown accustomed.

19 The Catch (and the Sweep)

Between 1921–1964, the New York Yankees captured the American League pennant 29 times. They won 20 of the 29 World Series in which they appeared during that span. Their most prolific stretch came in the middle of the century. The Yankees emerged victorious in seven games over the Brooklyn Dodgers in the 1947 Fall Classic. The Indians tied the Red Sox and won the subsequent one-game playoff for the pennant and edged the Yankees by two-and-a-half games in 1948 to advance to the World Series, which they won.

After that, however, the Yankees rattled off five consecutive titles. They seemed poised for a sixth straight, as they amassed 103 victories during the regular season, more than they tallied in any of the previous five years. The Tribe, however, totaled 111. Thus, Cleveland earned the right to square off—as a heavy favorite—against the New York Giants in the World Series.

"The Yankees had taken over baseball," said Bob DiBiasio, Indians senior vice president of public affairs. "People don't realize, the Yankees won every year except for '54."

That would hold true even after the '54 campaign. The Yankees reached the World Series in each of the following four seasons and nine of the ensuing 10. They fell short in '54, though, and the Indians instead sought their second championship in a seven-year span.

Willie Mays had other ideas.

Vic Wertz had his way with Giants starter Sal Maglie in Game 1. Cleveland's first baseman socked a two-run triple in the first inning and singles in the fourth and sixth. So when Maglie issued Larry Doby a free pass and served up a single to Al Rosen to begin the eighth, Giants skipper Leo Durocher opted for southpaw reliever Don Liddle to face the left-handed-hitting Wertz with the score tied 2–2.

Wertz delivered again, as he punished a ball to deep center, a spacious abyss at Polo Grounds. Mays had been playing a relatively shallow center field, so he had miles and miles of ground to cover as he chased after the soaring baseball. As gravity dragged the baseball toward the earth, Mays, his back turned to home plate, used his glove like a basket and hauled it in. His cap flew off as he twisted

The Hebrew Hammer

For about five years, Al Rosen was one of the most feared sluggers in the game. The Indians third baseman submitted one of the finest offensive single-season showings in franchise history in 1953. That year, one in which he took home the American League Most Valuable Player trophy, Rosen batted .336 with 43 home runs, 145 RBIs, and 115 runs scored. He came within one hit of winning the Triple Crown, as he lost the batting title by .001.

The next year, when the Indians captured the American League pennant, he hit .300 with 24 home runs. Rosen clubbed 156 round-trippers from 1950 to 1954. Nagging injuries ultimately limited his career to 10 seasons (seven full ones at the big league level), but he was a four-time All-Star and twice led the American League in home runs and RBIs. Rosen was inducted into the Indians Hall of Fame in 2006.

his body and fired a throw back toward the infield while he fell to the ground. Doby had to race back to second base, tag up and advance to third. The Indians failed to take the lead in the inning. The Giants proceeded to win 5–2 in 10 innings on a pinch-hit, three-run home run by Dusty Rhodes.

As Mays modestly quipped years later: "Everybody said, 'Well, it was a hard catch.' I said, 'It was an easy catch.'"

Mays did admit that he may have prevented a run from scoring. Given how far Wertz's shot took Mays, Doby might have been able to tag up and score from second had Mays not swiftly returned the ball to the infield. Mays said he could not see where he was throwing, but his frenzied heave was right on target to the cutoff man.

"The key there is catching the ball," Mays said, "and I think that hurt Cleveland very dearly. If I miss that ball, it might have been an inside-the-park home run. They could have scored easily. That was a big catch as far as the World Series was concerned."

Cleveland's bats remained dormant for the rest of the series, as the Indians scored only nine runs in the four games. A change in venue did not help. The Giants finished off the sweep at Cleveland Municipal Stadium. The Indians prevented the Yankees from winning another title, but they fell short in adding to their own collection.

20 World Series Walk-Off

For years upon years upon years, it was a slow, painful accumulation. Then, as the tide started turning and the team started winning, the breaths came more quickly and excitedly. When Eddie Murray delivered a single to center, the balloon popped. The air was released. Everyone let out a sigh of relief. The 47-year drought was over. The Indians had won a World Series game.

The 1995 campaign was like a dream. Tribe fans did not want to pinch themselves for fear of feeling nothing and realizing that it was all a mirage. The Indians had been so bad for so long. This could not be real. When the Indians claimed Game 3 of the World Series, that pinch became admissible. There was feeling there, plenty of it.

The Indians rolled into the World Series an offensive juggernaut, winners of a league-high 100 contests in the 144-game regular season. The Braves' dynamic starting pitching carved them down to size in the first two games at Atlanta-Fulton County Stadium. Greg Maddux, who earned his fourth consecutive National League Cy Young award for his 19–2 record and 1.63 ERA, tossed a complete game in the Braves' 3–2 Game 1 victory. Tom Glavine, who posted a 16–7 record and 3.08 ERA during the regular season, stymied the Tribe in a 4–3 win in Game 2.

Cleveland mustered only eight total hits in the first two tilts. The Indians collected 12 in Game 3. None was more significant than Murray's liner to center.

Murray approached the plate with the score tied 6–6 and no outs in the 11th inning. He had gone 0-for-5 with three strikeouts, but he had a chance to erase that from everyone's memory banks. Alvaro Espinoza stood at second base after pinch-running for Carlos Baerga, who commenced the inning with a double to right-center. Albert Belle stood at first following an intentional walk.

Murray attacked the first offering from Alejandro Pena, a fastball at the letters. Marquis Grissom's outfield throw sailed up the third-base line. Espinoza slid toward home and brushed the plate with his right hand.

"The Indians are back in the World Series!" Bob Costas shouted on the national telecast.

Six years after capturing a championship, the Indians were swept by the New York Giants in the 1954 World Series. Four decades of mostly misery ensued. Even after a magical regular season and first two rounds of the playoffs in 1995, the first two games of the Fall Classic seemed to serve as a reality check. Murray's walk-off single proved otherwise. Cleveland could exhale. This was no fantasy. It was real.

21 Comeback for the Ages

The Mariners ruled the regular season in 2001. They won a major league record-tying 116 games. The Athletics had to settle for the American League Wild Card because they tallied *only* 102 victories.

The Indians entered their tilt on August 5, 2001—a Sunday Night Baseball national telecast on ESPN—riding a three-game losing streak, a skid that dropped them to second place in the American League Central. They hosted Seattle at Jacobs Field before a sellout crowd of 42,494. Many of those fans bolted for the exits once the Mariners amassed a 12–0 advantage in the third inning.

The Mariners mounted an eight-run, seven-hit attack in the third, one inning after they plated four runs. Dave Burba departed before he could record an out in the third. Mike Bacsik didn't fare much better.

Bob DiBiasio, Indians vice president of public relations, had never taken a summer vacation with his wife and two kids. When Larry Dolan assumed ownership of the organization in 2001, he insisted that DiBiasio get away for a week and spend time with his family. So, the four traveled to Rehoboth Beach, Delaware, on August 5. They settled into their residence and DiBiasio tuned into the game.

By the time the seventh inning rolled around, DiBiasio's family had fallen asleep as the Mariners staked claim to a 14–2 lead. Both teams had pulled most of their starters. Center fielder Kenny Lofton recalled that he "wanted to stay in the game for some reason. Maybe I had a girlfriend there."

Russell Branyan commenced the bottom of the seventh with a solo home run. Two outs followed. Then, the floodgates opened. Einar Diaz singled to center and Lofton and Omar Vizquel walked. Jolbert Cabrera unloaded the bases with a two-run single. A three-run seventh closed the deficit to 14–5.

Eighth-inning home runs by Jim Thome and Marty Cordova shaved Seattle's lead to 14–8. Vizquel's RBI double made it 14–9. Still, the Indians needed five runs in the ninth to extend the affair. The Mariners' bullpen, anchored by closer Kazuhiro Sasaki and setup men Arthur Rhodes and Jeff Nelson, rarely crumbled.

Rhodes went 8–0 with a 1.72 ERA in 71 appearances, with 83 strikeouts in 68 innings. Nelson compiled a 2.76 ERA with 88 strikeouts in 65⅓ innings. Sasaki logged 45 saves.

"[Sasaki] used to have a *really* good split-finger," Vizquel said.

Eddie Taubensee led off the ninth with a single to center. Seattle's Norm Charlton retired Thome and Branyan, but Marty Cordova doubled and sent the southpaw to the showers. Nelson entered and walked Wil Cordero and served up a two-run single to Diaz. Lofton singled to left to load the bases.

Vizquel's 5-year-old son, Nico, was spending his first day as the team's bat boy. Now, his father was coming to the plate with

Eddie Taubensee hoists Kenny Lofton over his shoulder during a celebration after the Indians overcame a 12–0 deficit to beat the Mariners 15–14 on Sunday Night Baseball.

the bags packed with two outs in the ninth and his team trailing 14–11. The diminutive shortstop worked a full count and on the eighth pitch of the at-bat, he grounded a ball down the right-field line. The baseball trickled into the corner, past right fielder Charles Gipson. Cordero, Diaz, and Lofton all scored. Vizquel glided into third base and slapped hands with coach Joel Skinner, who then smacked Vizquel on the back of the helmet. Lofton repeatedly pumped his fists as he circled back to the dugout. It was delirium inside Jacobs Field.

"I'm screaming and waking everybody up and making them get out of bed and come to the TV," DiBiasio said. "My kids had no interest. They just wanted to sleep. So that's where I was when we came roaring back, sitting by myself in Delaware in a hotel on the beach."

The game proceeded until the 11th inning, when Lofton and Vizquel registered consecutive one-out singles. Jolbert Cabrera then splintered his bat on the first pitch from Jose Paniagua as he sent a soft liner into left field. Lofton sprinted around third and snuck his hand onto home plate before catcher Dan Wilson could apply the tag. Wilson stepped on Lofton's hand as the center fielder slid head-first across the dirt. Taubensee, who had been on deck, lifted Lofton over his shoulder as the Indians came pouring out of the dugout. The club congregated on the infield and went crazy. Vizquel lifted Nico up onto his shoulder as Lofton and Cabrera endured the celebratory wrath of their teammates.

In one controlled area of the ballpark: disbelief, shock, disappointment. Everywhere else: bedlam. The Indians became the first team in 76 years to overcome a 12-run deficit on their way to the 15–14 result. Over the final five innings, the Indians totaled 17 hits. Lofton and Vizquel each reached four times during that unfathomable stretch, with one walk and three hits apiece.

"It was one of the most exciting games I ever played in," Vizquel said. "I remember every minute of it."

22 Bang John Adams' Drum

If it weren't for a flock of perturbed teens, a timely beer run, and a bit of miscommunication, Progressive Field might be without its heartbeat.

On August 24, 1973, John Adams sat among the redwood bench seats in left field at Cleveland Municipal Stadium. It was common practice to smack the seats at the stadium to make noise. Adams had other ideas. He bought a drum set for $25. He has toted the 26-inch bass drum from that purchase to the ballpark for nearly every game ever since.

The Indians hosted the Texas Rangers on that Friday night. Adams sought permission from the organization, which granted him approval to lug the drum through the entrance gate as long as he didn't bother anyone with his banging. Adams often sat at the bottom of the bleachers. On this particular evening, a group of 16 high school kids, alternating boys and girls, sat in the row in front of him for a date night.

One of the boys in the group turned around and asked Adams: "You're not going to hit that, are you?" Adams relented and figured his plan was foiled. A man making a beer run passed Adams and asked if he was going to hit the drum. Adams told him he didn't want to bother anyone. So, the man directed him to the top of the bleachers in Section 55.

"You won't bother anybody up here," he said. "Come on."

Adams sat atop the bleachers and banged the drum. He went to work on Saturday, but returned with his drum on Sunday. A photographer from the Cleveland Press snapped a picture of him sitting with his instrument. Bob Sudyk, a reporter for the newspaper, called Adams at work on Monday and asked if he would be

John Adams can always be counted on to sit in the outfield bleachers and bang his drum at Indians home games.

attending Tuesday's tilt. Adams said he didn't plan on it. When the article was printed, however, it contained a different message toward the bottom: "If you want to hear John's drum, come to the game tonight."

"Not to make a liar out of the fifth estate, I said, 'Oh, why not?'" Adams said. "So I went down there that Tuesday night and Wednesday night and kept going down."

The club's promotions director, Jackie York, visited with Adams and asked if he would attend every home game. He politely declined her request, citing that he didn't want another obligation on his itinerary. He didn't follow through.

"I've come to virtually every game since," Adams said.

Adams' 3,000th game was on April 27, 2011. The Indians honored him three days later. They celebrated his 40th anniversary in August 2013. For the ceremonial first pitch, former second baseman Carlos Baerga tossed a baseball off of the drum. The ball caromed toward home plate.

The Indians treat Adams to four seats for every home game. He says he doesn't plan on ending the tradition until he can no longer make it up the steps to the top of the bleachers. He has patched up the drum's disintegrated rims. He had his neighbor weld together tension rods that had snapped. He has replaced the head and mallets, parts on which he estimates he spends about $200 each year.

For Adams, it's all worth it. He can recall sitting at the kitchen table of his childhood home in 1954, when his father finally agreed to take him to a game. They rode the Union Avenue bus downtown on Opening Day. They got off at the corner of E. 4th Street and Prospect Avenue, walked down Euclid Avenue and a large set of stairs until they could see the massive ballpark resting along the lake.

"Everything is just brick and asphalt and concrete," Adams said, "and then you walk into the place and when you walk up the ramp, everything is in color. I always think of that like when Dorothy in *The Wizard of Oz* opened the door and there were all of the vibrant colors, the blue sky, the green grass, the sounds, the smells. Every Opening Day, all of those memories come flooding back for me."

Baseball serves as Adams' escape from reality. He referred to Progressive Field as "a magical land," a place he meets his new best friends and watches real-life drama unfold on the diamond.

"You think you've seen it all until you see what you see next," he said. "That's the thrill of being there. It isn't predictable. It's drama, right there, in front of you, live, unscripted."

Fans venture his direction to greet him, take a picture with him, or thank him for his commitment. Maybe his popularity and

Bleacher Bums

It is the best spot to be before the game and it is one of the more unique places to experience an actual Indians game. The bleacher seats at Progressive Field are typically the most affordable and the most popular.

At Cleveland Stadium, fans would bang on the metal seats to make noise and give off the feeling that there were 50,000 fans in attendance rather than the 5,000 or so that usually scattered throughout the cavernous venue on a nightly basis. The bleachers at Progressive Field are the only metal seats remaining in the building. A series of long, metal benches span the 19-foot-high wall in left field underneath the scoreboard.

John Adams sits atop the middle section of the bleachers with his 26-inch bass drum, in the same position he has occupied since August 1973. Fans often swarm the railing that sits at the bottom of the area for batting practice, as hitters spray fly balls in that direction.

perception result from when people think about him and his drum. When the instrument is its loudest, at its peak, the Indians are typically performing well. Subconsciously, fans associate the rapid strikes of the drum with a run-scoring hit or a game-saving double play. A few seconds before the opposing hurler heaves a pitch that an Indians player clubs for a walk-off home run, all anyone can hear is the steady beat of the drum.

Adams has met fans from every continent on the planet, save for Antarctica, though he said he waits for the day a penguin moseys up the steps to visit him in his signature spot. He met a family from Hong Kong. He met a guy from Austria who made the trip on the recommendation of his father. He took a picture with a family from Paris, France, another from South Korea, and others from Denmark and Japan. Adams said he doesn't understand the adulation, but he appreciates it. He suggests he's just a fan with an avid interest in rooting on his team.

After all, if it wasn't for that man making a beer run or the cost-efficient $25 price on that drum set or the miscommunication with the Cleveland Press reporter, perhaps Adams wouldn't have established the daily tradition. But, as he notes, sometimes unplanned events work out better than those that are mapped out.

Said Adams: "Am I not the luckiest guy in the world?"

23 Slim Jim

Even when the lanky, 21-year-old third baseman lifted Steve Farr's 1-0 offering into the deserted upper deck in right field at Yankee Stadium, no one could have envisioned what was to come for the kid sporting a No. 6 jersey. Jim Thome's first career home run, on October 4, 1991, the third-to-last day of the regular season, provided the last-place Indians with a victory against the Bronx Bombers.

"He didn't stand out like, 'This guy is going to be a Hall of Famer,'" said Indians team president Mark Shapiro. "He just clearly had incredible power. He was strong and much more athletic than people give him credit for."

Thome proceeded to club 11 career home runs at Yankee Stadium, one of 38 ballparks in which he trotted around the bases. He deposited 190 pitches over the fences at Progressive Field. Farr became the first of 403 different pitchers tagged by Thome for a tater. He teed off against Roger Clemens eight times and Justin Verlander seven times. He victimized Rick Reed on nine occasions in 27 career at-bats, including seven times in 16 at-bats during the 2002 campaign, in which he slugged a career-high 52 round-trippers.

He hit home runs for five different teams and against 30 different teams. He registered 48 multi-homer games, including a pair of three-homer affairs. Of his 612 career home runs, nine came with the bases loaded and 337 came with the bases empty. The fourth inning was his favorite (90 home runs), but he wasn't picky. He totaled at least 38 home runs in each of the nine innings. His final blast came against Toronto hurler Carlos Villanueva on September 26, 2012, a mere 7,664 days after his first career long ball. He swatted his 610th and 611th home runs against the Indians, the team with which he spent the majority of his career.

From his infamous batting stance, in which he pointed his bat to the sky above center field, he made a habit out of sending majestic drives into the stands. That stance is now permanently entrenched at Progressive Field in the form of a statue that stands tall beyond the center field wall.

For a while, such recognition of Thome near Lake Erie seemed implausible. Upon hitting the free agent market after the 2002 campaign and insisting that fans would have to "rip the uniform off of my back" for him to bolt Cleveland, Thome did just that. He ventured to greener pastures in Philadelphia, where the Phillies lured him with a six-year, $87 million commitment—a more enticing offer than the Indians' five-year, $62 million submission. The Indians, who had just initiated a rebuilding process, received a sucker punch to the gut with the loss of their offensive cornerstone.

"In life, you're always going to say things that ultimately you look back when you get older and say, 'You know what, maybe those weren't the right choice of words,'" Thome said. "I always envisioned that I was going to remain an Indian and when it didn't happen, it's not something that I look back on and say, 'I wish I would've made this decision or that decision.' When you make decisions, you move forward, but maybe some choice of words you do regret a little bit. I think you learn from them. You do make mistakes in life."

Thome contributed to the Indians' magical run of dominance from 1995–2001, a period during which the Tribe claimed six American League Central Division titles and appeared in two Fall Classics. Thome himself earned trips to the All-Star Game in 1997, '98, and '99, as he shared the field with many of his Indians teammates. He didn't stick around for the trying times, however. With the Indians in a downturn and the club unwilling to extend as lucrative an offer in his direction, he opted to leave town. The country boy, born and raised in Peoria, Illinois, who had spent his years with the Tribe living in a quiet community on a golf course in the suburbs, took the money and ran.

The departure left a bitter taste in the mouths of the fans who watched him total 334 home runs during his 12 years in Cleveland. He provided power when it mattered most. He socked the go-ahead home run in Game 5 of the 1995 American League Championship Series against Seattle. He hit the game-tying home run in Game 1 and a pair of two-run home runs in Game 5 of the 1999 American League Division Series against Boston. In all, he totaled 17 postseason long balls.

Against Royals hurler Don Wengert, he clobbered a home run that traveled a ballpark-record 511 feet on July 3, 1999. The baseball landed in the plaza beyond center field and bounced onto Eagle Avenue, the street that runs adjacent to the left-field bleachers, behind the stadium.

"Jim Thome has just left Jacobs Field, onto Eagle Avenue," radio announcer Tom Hamilton described. "That will take two tape measures."

He established a new club record with a total of 52 home runs in his final season in Cleveland. He eclipsed Albert Belle's mark of 50, set in 1995, with his 51st blast on September 27, 2002.

"If you go to a game, you don't want to go eat when he's hitting," said Indians manager Terry Francona, "because those are majestic. He takes some pretty healthy swings."

Thome's career came to a close after he amassed 612 home runs over 22 seasons. He tallied 2,328 hits, 1,699 RBIs, 1,747 walks, 2,548 strikeouts, and five All-Star Game nods. He entered the majors with the Indians a week after reaching the legal drinking age as a skinny third baseman. He finished his career with the Orioles as a 42-year-old with a balky back, a guy limited to part-time

Back at the Hot Corner

The night before the Indians' final home game in 2011, manager Manny Acta couldn't sleep. His racing mind spawned a creative notion. He presented his idea to the masses in the ninth inning of Cleveland's contest against Minnesota at Progressive Field on September 25.

Jim Thome, acquired by the Tribe one month earlier, pinch-hit for Shelley Duncan in the bottom of the eighth. In the ensuing frame, Thome's last at home as a member of the Indians, the 41-year-old trotted out to third base, the position he manned when he entered the league two decades earlier.

"I just felt that if this is the end—at least with our franchise—I thought it was proper that he end where he started—at third base," Acta said after the game.

Thome hadn't played third base since September 29, 1996. When the Indians traded for Matt Williams prior to the 1997 campaign, Thome shifted across the diamond to first. By 2011, Thome hadn't played the field at all in four years and hadn't played defense regularly since 2004.

"To get that opportunity to go back out there, it felt really good," Thome said. "Just like old times."

After one pitch by Joe Smith to Trevor Plouffe, Thome retreated to the dugout before a standing ovation. Acta had instructed Smith to toss a pitch out of Plouffe's reach to be safe, but he actually threw the Twins' third baseman a strike. Minnesota skipper Ron Gardenhire said he was hoping Plouffe would bunt the ball toward Thome.

The veteran, who was using infielder Jack Hannahan's glove, would have welcomed the action.

"I would have made the play," Thome said.

designated hitter duties because of his body's limitations and the mileage accumulated over two decades in the league.

Before he finally called it a career, he mended a fence that had been hanging open in his mind for years. On August 25, 2011, the Indians paid the Minnesota Twins $20,000 to acquire Thome. Cleveland had surprisingly hung around in the American League Central race. Before the Detroit Tigers completely ran away with the division, the Indians opted to make one, final transaction in an effort to occupy a spot in an injury-riddled lineup, give the team a late-summer boost and fill Progressive Field with a month-long dose of nostalgia.

Thome arrived in Cleveland the following day, a Friday. He traversed every inch of the ballpark, reconnecting with old friends and colleagues. The Indians drew more than 100,000 fans to the stadium the weekend of his return. In his first game back with the Tribe, Thome batted fourth.

"The memories, the excitement of the fans, seeing them embrace me," Thome said. "I didn't know if I would ever get that opportunity to watch that again and see that excitement."

Thome said he doesn't have any regrets. He routinely imagined how a return to an Indians uniform would go over. He played out the scenarios, but never really considered them a possibility. When he knew he was Cleveland-bound in August 2011, he became overly anxious. He wasn't sure if the fans would embrace him.

"That first night when I got introduced and the crowd cheered me, it's something I'll never forget," Thome said. "You leave a place and ultimately you want to be accepted back. I appreciate the fact that they did accept me back and give me that opportunity and cheered."

The Indians celebrated Thome's birthday on August 27, 2011, as the man enjoying his 41st birthday played his second game with his old club. In the sixth inning, Thome slugged a game-tying home run off of Kansas City's Danny Duffy. The ball landed in the bleacher seats in left-center field. It marked the 602nd home run of his career.

"I have a different view of him in hindsight than I did when he was playing here," Shapiro said. "He is one of those guys that the longer you're in the game, the more you appreciate how special he is. Back then, he just seemed like an incredibly nice, genuine, innocent guy who was incredibly strong and had a lot of talent. Looking back, his humility and ability to treat people so incredibly well in light of the talent he had and what he was on the verge of accomplishing was pretty remarkable."

On August 2, 2014, the Indians unveiled a gold statue of Thome near Heritage Park in center field at the ballpark. The likeness displays the slugger commencing his batting ritual, with his lumber pointed out into the abyss. Also on that cloudy Saturday afternoon, Thome signed a one-day contract with the Indians and officially retired as a member of the organization that had drafted him in the 13th round out of Illinois Central College a quarter-century earlier.

He left his mark with his teammates.

"He doesn't act like he's above anybody," said Sandy Alomar Jr. "It shows young players that you don't have to be this different type of guy to be a star player."

He left his mark on the league.

"He's a guy who has been so honest and truthful to the game," said Omar Vizquel. "He's the image people want to follow."

He left his mark with team executives.

"You talk about a guy who represented your organization with class and dignity and integrity," said Bob DiBiasio, Indians senior vice president of public affairs. "Just the wholesomeness, the purity, at a time when you learned that other people were not."

And he penned the final chapter of his career with the organization in which it all started.

"When the statue got closer, it was important for me to do this during this time," Thome said. "I wanted to retire an Indian. It's a dream come true."

24 The One That Wasn't

There was always a reason. An excuse, maybe, but that term diminishes what the Indians did, in fact, accomplish in the '90s. Still, there was always some obstacle that prevented the club from cementing itself in the pantheon of elite teams. Are the 1995 Indians one of the greatest teams in baseball history? Certainly. They won 100 games (out of 144) during the regular season and reached the World Series. But—and there was always a "but" during that era of Tribe baseball—they fell short in the end. They could not compete with the Atlanta Braves' stout starting pitching. The umpires, some say, gave Greg Maddux and Co. a bit of extra wiggle room as well.

In 1996, the Indians won 99 games and seemed poised for a repeat trip to the Fall Classic, but in the American League Division Series, they could not keep the Orioles in the ballpark. Baltimore blasted nine home runs and captured the series in four games. The Indians boasted a balanced team in 1998. They bounced Boston in the first round. But they ran into the New York Yankees in the American League Championship Series. Joe Torre's squad tallied 114 victories during the regular season. No one was going to stop them in October, either. The Indians handed them their only two postseason defeats, but fell in six games.

The Indians lacked sufficient pitching in 1999 and 2000. In '99, they became the first team in the modern era to score 1,000 runs. Five players crossed home plate at least 100 times. But pitching signed the season's death warrant. In the first two tilts of the American League Division Series, Tribe hurlers held the Red Sox to a total of three runs on 11 hits. Over the next three contests, however, Boston tallied 44 runs on 45 hits to send Cleveland packing. Pitching plagued the Indians again in 2000 and the club finished one game short in the race for a playoff berth.

The 1997 season was different. The Indians did not compile a triple-digit win total. They did not cruise to another American League Central division crown. It did not appear as though there would need to be an excuse. The team simply did not seem good enough to merit one.

Of course, that all changed the second Tony Fernandez's 11th-inning blast landed in the right-field seats at Camden Yards. Jose Mesa polished off the Orioles in the bottom half of the frame and the Indians headed to South Beach as the heavy favorites in a World Series matchup against the Florida Marlins.

Despite their uninspiring regular season and close calls against the Yankees and Orioles in October, the Indians were still playing in their second Fall Classic in a three-year span. They had the experience, the hunger. The Marlins had assembled a veteran-laden squad, but they had only been a franchise since 1993. They were attempting to become the first Wild Card team to win the sport's top prize. No one could have seen it coming back in June or July, when the Indians were floundering around the .500 mark, but this time, there would not be an excuse, no additional reasoning necessary for another letdown. This was the best opportunity for a title.

Game 1

Livan Hernandez, then a 22-year-old rookie with 17 regular season starts under his belt, out-pitched Orel Hershiser, who made his big league debut when Hernandez was 8. Back-to-back home runs by

Moises Alou and Charles Johnson did in Hershiser, who suffered the loss.

Final: Marlins 7, Indians 4

Game 2

Chad Ogea, nearly named the Most Valuable Player of the series, limited Florida to one run over 6⅔ innings. Bip Roberts (two-run single) and Sandy Alomar Jr. (two-run home run) provided the offensive lift.

Final: Indians 6, Marlins 1

Game 3

The series shifted to the arctic tundra known as Jacobs Field and the starting pitchers, Al Leiter and Charles Nagy, were wild and rather ineffective. They issued a combined 10 free passes. The Indians grabbed a 7–3 lead on Jim Thome's two-run home run in the fifth, but the Marlins responded with 11 runs over the final four frames, including seven in a sloppy, error-filled ninth. Cleveland mounted a four-run rally in its last gasp, but to no avail.

Final: Marlins 14, Indians 11

Game 4

Snow flurries scattered from the sky during batting practice and pregame routines and the temperature hovered around freezing for much of the contest. The Indians' bats were plenty warm, however. Cleveland pounded out 15 hits and rookie hurler Jaret Wright improved to 3–0 in the postseason.

Final: Indians 10, Marlins 3

Game 5

Hernandez again outperformed Hershiser, as Alou tagged the veteran righty for another three-run blast. The Indians chipped away at Florida's four-run lead in the ninth, but Alomar—who had four RBIs in the game—flied out with two outs and the tying run on base.

Final: Marlins 8, Indians 7

Game 6

Not only did Ogea hold the Marlins to one run in five innings, but he plated a pair of runs with a second-inning single. The Tribe bullpen patched together four scoreless frames to send the series to a decisive affair.

Final: Indians 4, Marlins 1

Game 7

Hargrove opted for Wright on short rest in place of Nagy and the youngster delivered. He allowed only one hit through six innings and held Florida scoreless until Bobby Bonilla took him deep to start the seventh. Still, the Indians gripped a 2–1 lead into the ninth inning. Jose Mesa could not shut the door on the franchise's first championship in 39 years, though. He served up a pair of singles and Craig Counsell tied the game with a sacrifice fly to the warning track in right field. In the 11th, after a single and a Fernandez error, Edgar Renteria supplied the title-clinching single up the middle off the tip of Nagy's glove.

Final: Marlins 3, Indians 2

"Sometimes that empty feeling is there, because you haven't achieved the ultimate goal," said Bob DiBiasio, Indians senior vice president for public affairs.

There is no reasonable answer for the 1997 shortcoming. There was no glaring disadvantage. Maybe they never should have been on that stage in the first place, after an 86-win regular season. But they were. They never got closer. It is as close as any team possibly could get.

"I think we're all driven by it," said team president Mark Shapiro. "I think we all share disappointment that we haven't done it, period, whether it was then or now or whenever. But I don't think that diminishes what was an incredible run of Indians baseball with some incredibly talented teams."

25 The Curse of Rocky Colavito

Rocky Colavito just wanted the day to end. Not only did he go hitless with four strikeouts in six at-bats—the only four-whiff game of his 14-year big league career—but the tension and uneasiness were overwhelming. It was April 19, 1960. It was two days after Easter Sunday, two days after he switched allegiances, and two days after the latest show-stopping swap executed by Indians general manager Frank "Trader" Lane, a man who derived pleasure out of dealing star players.

Colavito led the American League with 42 home runs in 1959. A year earlier, he hit .303 with 41 home runs and 113 RBIs. In 1959, he earned a trip to two All-Star Games and finished in the top four in balloting for the American League Most Valuable Player award for the second consecutive season. That year, he set a franchise record (and tied the big league mark) with four home runs in one game on June 10, 1959. Yet two days before the commencement of the 1960 regular season, Lane shipped Colavito to Detroit in exchange for Harvey Kuenn, the 1959 batting champion who had logged a .353 average for the Tigers.

Lane and Colavito had engaged in a contract squabble, but the powerful right fielder was the face of the franchise and a fan favorite. Kuenn was a nice player, a singles and doubles hitter and a perennial All-Star. He never whacked more than 12 home runs in a season, however. And Colavito was just reaching his prime, at the age of 26. Tribe fans were not fond of the deal. They would support it even less as time went on.

Lane had built a reputation as a quick-trigger trader, an executive who would not come to regret his exchanges years later, only because he said the trades he did regret were the ones he did not make. He made 60 deals in a two-year span from December 1957–1959. He dealt away Roger Maris in 1958. Three years later, Maris established a new major league single-season home run record. Lane acquired first baseman Norm Cash from the Chicago White Sox following the 1959 campaign. However, before Cash ever suited up for the Indians, he was sent to the Tigers. Cash proceeded to slug 373 home runs for Detroit. The player Cleveland received in return, Steve Demeter, totaled five hitless at-bats for the Indians. Five days before Colavito was traded to the Tigers, Cash joined the club. Cash, 25 years old at the time, would spend the final 15 years of his career with Detroit.

Kuenn played only one season in Cleveland before he, too, was traded. One month before Lane left his position, he dealt Kuenn to the San Francisco Giants for pitcher Johnny Antonelli and outfielder Willie Kirkland. Antonelli appeared in 11 games with the Indians and posted an 0–4 record and 6.56 ERA. Kirkland pieced together three forgettable years with the club, as he logged a .232 batting average and 63 home runs.

The Indians had amassed an 89–65 record in 1959, good for second place in the American League. Once they traded away Colavito, "The Curse of Rocky Colavito" set in. For the next 34 years, the Indians finished better than fourth place just once: a third-place finish in 1968.

Gabe Paul wanted to make things right. Lane was gone and Paul, always one to fawn over and attempt to lure stars, ran the front office. So, prior to the 1965 season, the Indians reacquired

Colavito in a three-team deal involving the White Sox and the Kansas City Athletics. Cleveland parted with southpaw Tommy John, who had amassed a 2–9 record and 3.91 ERA as a 21-year-old the year before. He proceeded to pitch for another 24 years. By the time he retired, he had tallied 288 wins. The Indians also sent away 22-year-old outfielder Tommie Agee, who had played sparingly with the Tribe. He won the American League Rookie of the Year award with Chicago in 1966, made two All-Star teams and garnered a pair of Gold Glove awards. Catcher John Romano, a two-time All-Star for Cleveland, also departed.

Colavito came back to Cleveland and registered two more All-Star seasons. He was on the downside of his career, though. By 1967, he was washed up and the Indians traded him to the White Sox. The curse lived on.

26 The 180-Foot Dash

No one remembers Ruben Amaro scoring first. Kenny Lofton's mad dash around half of the diamond is all anyone recalls about the victory that propelled the Indians to their first World Series appearance in 41 years.

The Indians arrived at the Kingdome on October 17, 1995, grasping a 3–2 advantage over the Mariners in the American League Championship Series. Seattle sent southpaw Randy Johnson to the hill in an attempt to salvage its season. Cleveland countered with Dennis Martinez. The hurlers delivered a classic pitcher's duel that left the contest hanging in the balance until an unforgettable eighth inning.

Tony Pena opened the frame with a double to right-center. Amaro replaced him on the basepaths. Then, Lofton put on a clinic and, in a short sequence, demonstrated the value of elite speed.

Lofton bunted to the right of the pitcher's mound and beat it out for a single. Amaro advanced to third on the play. On the next pitch, the first offering to Omar Vizquel, Lofton swiped second base. Two pitches later, Johnson's heater caromed off the mitt of catcher Dan Wilson and trickled past the visitors' on-deck circle.

Amaro jogged home with ease. Lofton dashed to third, but never hesitated or slowed down. He rounded the bag and bolted to the plate. The Mariners didn't anticipate his aggressiveness. Johnson was ill-prepared to cover home. Wilson couldn't retrieve the ball in a swift enough manner. Lofton scored from second on a passed ball. The Indians plated a pair of critical, late-inning runs without a swing of the bat. The passed ball turned the Indians' 1–0 edge into a seemingly insurmountable 3–0 advantage.

Not only did Lofton never slow down while rounding third base, he also never pumped his brakes after he crossed the plate. The visitors' dugout at the Kingdome was split into two halves, separated by an opening that led into a large space that fed into the clubhouse. In the large space sat batting tees and a cage. Lofton's dash took him through the opening and down toward the dugout. There, he ran into traveling secretary Mike Seghi and vice president of public relations Bob DiBiasio, who pushed him back into the swarm of players who had followed him.

"That has forever demonstrated how he can impact the game," said team president Mark Shapiro. "It's that or it's the catch in center field here when he went halfway up the wall and the top of the wall was literally below waist-high so he could go up and catch the ball. Those two just made you think that there's nothing out of the realm of possibilities with him on the field, nothing that he couldn't do."

Kenny Lofton scores from second around the tag of Randy Johnson on a passed ball as the Indians mounted a win in the 1995 ALCS and advanced to the World Series.

After Vizquel lined out to left, Carlos Baerga tacked on one, final run with a solo home run. Cleveland captured a 4–0 victory and moved on to the Fall Classic to face the Atlanta Braves.

"I can see it in my mind like it was yesterday, Kenny Lofton dashing home from second base in the Kingdome," said Indians radio announcer Tom Hamilton. "You knew then that they were going to win the World Series. First off, nobody scores from second on a passed ball. To do it against Randy Johnson—he didn't like Kenny Lofton anyway and Kenny didn't like Randy Johnson—it was just poetic justice.

"You remember those kinds of moments."

27 A Most Unfortunate Pitch

On a wall in Heritage Park at Progressive Field rests a bronze plaque that carries the legacy of a man who suffered baseball's greatest on-field tragedy. On August 16, 1920, at Polo Grounds, New York Yankees hurler Carl Mays struck Indians shortstop Ray Chapman in the head. Chapman died hours later. Toward the bottom of the plaque reads a message: "He Lives In The Hearts Of All Who Knew Him."

The plaque was first displayed at League Park. It was relocated to Cleveland Stadium when the Indians moved into the new space. Eventually, it was taken down until employees unearthed the piece of history in a storage room at Jacobs Field in February 2007. The fading plaque was restored and placed in Heritage Park. It notes that Chapman was known for his "inspiring enthusiasm, cheerfulness and unfailing loyalty to his club."

It is an important piece of Indians lore. Surely, no one wants to pore over the details of Chapman's untimely, unfathomable death. But the shortstop—known for his dazzling defense, speed on the bases, and sacrifice bunting skill—deserves to be remembered and honored appropriately for his contributions with his bat, glove, and legs.

It was common practice for pitchers to scuff a baseball before throwing a pitch. Mays delivered the ball with a submarine style, the fingers on his right hand nearly scraping the dirt. Chapman's lack of a reaction to the ball buzzing its way toward his dome indicates he never saw the flight of the dirtied orb. The intensity of the impact had Mays thinking the ball had collided with Chapman's bat, so the pitcher fielded the ball and tossed it to first. Chapman collapsed to the ground and was helped off the field. Yankees manager Miller Huggins signaled for a pair of doctors sitting in the stands. Chapman died early the following morning in St. Lawrence Hospital in New York City.

Fans gathered at Grand Central Station as Chapman's body was transported back to Cleveland. Thousands congregated for his funeral on August 20 as they commemorated the career and life of a man who had blossomed into one of Cleveland's cornerstones. In his eight full big league seasons, Chapman batted .300 or better on three occasions. He scored at least 75 runs six times. He stole 20 or more bases six times. He tallied at least 10 triples four times.

Chapman was a fan favorite and was beloved by his teammates. He was close friends with manager Tris Speaker, with whom he played from 1916–1920. The Indians canceled their affair with the Yankees the day after the incident occurred. When they returned to the field on August 18, they proceeded to lose seven of nine games and their grip on first place in the American League. They rallied, however, as Joe Sewell, an eventual member of the Baseball Hall of Fame, assumed Chapman's spot in the lineup. The Indians captured the pennant and knocked off the Brooklyn Robins to win the World Series.

Following the 1920 campaign, spitballs—a Mays specialty—were banned. Umpires were also required to incorporate unused, clean baseballs into action more regularly.

Chapman was inducted into the Indians Hall of Fame in 2006.

28 A Series to Remember

The 1997 American League Championship Series, which pitted the Orioles against the Indians, was jam-packed full of costly errors, bizarre mishaps, and season-altering home runs. By the end of the series, after Jose Mesa shut down the Orioles in the bottom of the 11th in Game 6, the Indians were wiped.

More than anything, though, they were just ready to leave Baltimore for the sunny shores of South Florida, where the Florida Marlins awaited their World Series competitor. And it made no sense to fly to Cleveland and then fly down south a day later, so the team departed for Miami the next morning, mere hours after Tony Fernandez penned the final act of an adventurous American League Championship Series script with a game-winning home run in the 11th inning. After Game 6, the team hotel closed down and held a private party for everyone associated with the Indians, as they toasted their second Fall Classic appearance in three years. Pitcher Brian Anderson, a native of Geneva, Ohio, sat with his mother and father and recounted the time he told his parents he was going to help a Cleveland team win a championship some day after the three watched Earnest Byner fumble away Cleveland's hopes at a trip to the Super Bowl in January 1988. Anderson earned the victory in Game 6 of the American League Championship Series. Players, coaches, spouses, families, and team executives drank beer and reminisced through the night.

Some grew hungry. Broadcasters Tom Hamilton and Matt Underwood joined vice president of public relations Bob DiBiasio for a late-night excursion. They figured there was no point in venturing upstairs to their rooms, sleeping for a couple of hours and then catching the bus to the airport. They might as well stay awake.

They could sleep on the plane and on the beach upon their arrival. Plus, they were famished. The three walked the streets of Baltimore in the middle of the night, in search of an establishment that was open and serving food. They meandered through the streets of downtown as the clock pushed 3:00 AM. They finally came across a diner that was open. They walked in and people gazed at them. Two cops were sitting down. One approached the trio and asked what they were doing. They told him they worked for the Indians.

"Oh yeah? You broke our hearts tonight," the cop said. He glanced at a lady working behind the counter and said: "I don't know if she'll serve you."

He then asked how they got to the restaurant. They replied that they walked from the team hotel.

"Are you guys fucking stupid?" he said, before lecturing them about the dangers of downtown Baltimore late at night. He waited for them as they ate their food and called them a cab to take them back to the hotel.

"To this day, we're like, 'We were just looking for cheeseburgers and milkshakes,'" DiBiasio said.

"That's one of my fondest memories," Hamilton said.

After a series filled with nauseating drama, who could blame them for wanting a satisfying meal?

The Orioles claimed Game 1, 3–0, behind eight shutout innings from Scott Erickson. The Indians went quietly, managing only four singles and no walks. Brady Anderson, on the other hand, slugged Chad Ogea's first pitch of the game over the right-field fence.

Baltimore held a 4–2 lead in the eighth inning of Game 2 when Armando Benitez walked Sandy Alomar Jr. and Jim Thome. With two outs, Marquis Grissom, who replaced All-Star center fielder Kenny Lofton in Cleveland just before the season began, delivered a go-ahead three-run home run. The long ball reversed the course of the series.

All of the wackiness came to light in Game 3 at Jacobs Field. Despite Mike Mussina's American League Championship Series-record 15 strikeouts in seven innings, the Indians grasped a 1–0 advantage in the ninth inning when Jeffrey Hammonds sent a dribbler to second base. Tony Fernandez gathered the baseball and attempted to tag Jeff Reboulet, who was running from first to second, but Reboulet dropped to the ground at Fernandez's feet and avoided the tag. Fernandez threw to first to retire Hammonds and Thome tried to throw back to second to get Reboulet. But the throw hit Reboulet's left arm, so the Orioles had a runner on second with one out.

Anderson then skied a fly ball to center field. As gravity pulled the ball back toward the outfield grass, Grissom stuck out his arms and signaled that he did not see it. The ball landed beyond Grissom and left fielder Brian Giles sprinted over and slid to the ground to corral it. Reboulet scored with ease and Anderson trotted into second as the Orioles tied the game.

Grissom got redemption. He drew a one-out walk in the 12th inning and advanced to third on a single to right by Fernandez. On a 2-1 pitch, Omar Vizquel squared to lay down a squeeze bunt as Grissom bolted for the plate. Vizquel missed the ball as his momentum carried him up the first-base line. The ball skimmed off the glove of catcher Lenny Webster, who thought Vizquel had foul tipped it. Grissom crossed the plate as Webster leisurely picked up the ball and home-plate umpire John Hirschbeck motioned his arms to make a safe call. Vizquel jumped up and down, Orioles manager Davey Johnson rushed out of his dugout to argue and the Indians spilled out of their dugout to greet Grissom, who had atoned for his lost ball in the ninth inning by winning the game with a controversial steal of home.

Another walk-off propelled the Indians to a 3–1 series lead, as Alomar delivered a game-winning RBI single in Game 4, moments after the Orioles had tagged Jose Mesa with his second straight blown save. Baltimore staved off elimination with a 4–2 win in Game 5, but Fernandez's 11th-inning blast in Game 6 broke a scoreless tie and catapulted Cleveland into the Fall Classic.

The Orioles outscored the Indians, 19–18, and outhit the Indians, 54–40, in the series, but timely hitting—and a steal of home—lifted the Tribe to a nutty series victory.

29 Hold Up

It might not have made a difference. After all, the Red Sox surged to an 11–2 victory and advanced to the World Series, a clash with the Colorado Rockies that ended in four games.

It probably will never be forgotten, though.

Would Kenny Lofton have scored? Would the momentum have turned the tide in the decisive game? Would the Indians have bested Colorado in the Fall Classic as handily as Boston did?

Revisionist history is a funny thing. Hindsight is 20/20, but Indians fans don't always prefer to look at Joel Skinner's coaching career through anything but foggy goggles.

The Indians grabbed a commanding 3–1 series lead in the 2007 American League Championship Series, thanks to strong starting pitching by Jake Westbrook and Paul Byrd and a slew of timely hitting. Josh Beckett pitched Boston to a Game 5 victory at Jacobs Field with eight dominant innings and 11 strikeouts.

The series shifted back to Fenway Park for Game 6, a contest in which the Red Sox breezed to a lopsided win. That set the table for Game 7, with the Tribe reeling and the Red Sox salivating about the thought of a second World Series appearance in a four-year span.

Boston staked claim to a 3–2 lead as the teams reached the seventh inning. Hideki Okajima retired Jhonny Peralta on a fly out to right field. Kenny Lofton reached first and advanced to second on an error. Franklin Gutierrez then roped a base hit over the third-base bag. The baseball caromed off the green wall that juts out in foul territory in shallow left field. As Manny Ramirez trotted in to corral the loose ball, Lofton scurried around the third-base bag.

But there stood Skinner, both of his arms raised, his body sending a forceful message to Lofton, instructing the speedster to stop in his tracks.

Lofton slammed on the brakes and retreated to third base. Skinner shook Lofton's hand, patted him on the back with his left hand and pointed to where the ball had ricocheted as he explained his reasoning for holding him.

Initially, Skinner had waved Lofton toward home, his left arm rapidly spiraling like a pinwheel. As Lofton approached the base, with Ramirez bearing down on the stray baseball, Skinner changed his mind. At the moment Lofton rounded third base, Ramirez was four steps shy of the ball. He eventually scooped it up with his bare hand and tossed it into the infield. By then, however, Lofton had been denied a chance to score.

The give and take between announcers Joe Buck and Tim McCarver conveyed the element of surprise about Lofton being held at third.

Buck: "Lofton will round third. He's STOPPED. And it's first and third, one out."

McCarver: "What is that all about?…There is no way that Manny, in my judgement—and Joe, evidently in yours—that he even would have had a play. He'd probably go to second base with the ball."

On the first pitch of the ensuing at-bat, Casey Blake grounded into an inning-ending, momentum-squashing, series-altering double play.

Sing Along

The Indians stood one win away from a ticket to the World Series. They had one game remaining at Jacobs Field. If the Boston Red Sox captured Game 5 of the 2007 American League Championship Series, the series would shift back to Fenway Park.

So, the Indians pulled out all of the stops for Game 5 in an attempt to deliver their fans a postseason series victory at home. It was all unintentional, of course. Or so the Indians claimed.

Singer Taylor Swift was slated to sing the National Anthem prior to Game 5, but backed out. The Indians replaced her with country singer Danielle Peck. Shortly after the announcement of the musical revision, the Indians learned Peck was the ex-girlfriend of Red Sox pitcher Josh Beckett, who just so happened to be Boston's starter for Game 5.

Peck grew up in Coshocton, Ohio, about a two-hour drive from the Indians' ballpark. She was a Tribe fan. And she watched her ex-boyfriend pitch a gem. Beckett tallied 11 strikeouts in eight innings, as the Red Sox recorded a 7–1 triumph. They would proceed to win the remaining games of the series and sweep the Colorado Rockies in the Fall Classic.

The Indians pleaded ignorance with regards to Beckett and Peck's prior relationship. Beckett abrasively thanked the Indians for flying a friend to the game so she could watch his performance free of charge.

"It's tough to read if it's ricocheting back to the shortstop or to left-center," Tribe manager Eric Wedge said after the game. "I think it was just a tough read for [Skinner]."

Skinner never received publicized blame from anyone on the Indians or anyone involved with that game, though many agree Lofton would have undoubtedly scored.

"I think it gets overblown," said team president Mark Shapiro, then the club's general manager. "You could argue Kenny could see that on his own or know the ballpark. There's not any one player or one moment that is single-handedly responsible for us winning or losing."

The Red Sox eventually tagged Tribe reliever Rafael Betancourt for seven runs (six earned) to remove any doubt from the outcome.

Terry Francona served as Boston's manager for that enthralling seven-game series. In October 2012, he took over the reins as the Indians' skipper. He was once asked about Skinner's decision.

"Being a third-base coach in Boston is probably the most unfair job in the world," Francona said, "because you're making a split-second decision, and you're the only one in the ballpark who can't see the whole field, because you get that blind spot down the left-field line, and the ball caroms off the wall like it did in that instance—I think what you have to hope for is you have to make that split-second decision. What we used to tell our runners was, 'Keep your head up, like on a swivel, so you can be your own coach.' Because that happens more often than people realize.... If the runner keeps his head up, then he can score on his own and you don't run into that problem, because the third-base coach is in a real bind there."

That play doesn't claw at Shapiro any longer, but the series as a whole still stings.

"Certain things are less and less over time. That one is more and more," Shapiro said. "They were the best team in baseball, but we had them on the ropes. We had them down 3–1 and we had CC [Sabathia], Fausto [Carmona], and Westbrook pitching and we couldn't get a win. You kind of felt like once we went back into their place, anything could happen. That one is tough to get past. Getting in the World Series would have been great, and in these jobs you don't spend a ton of time dwelling on it, but that one doesn't get easy to get past."

30 In the Nick of Father Time

The Indians closed the 2013 campaign with 10 consecutive wins. They needed all 10 to earn the right to host the American League Wild Card Game. A handful of the victories came in dicey fashion, though none more demanding than a 5–4 triumph against the Chicago White Sox on September 24.

The Indians handed closer Chris Perez a 3–2 advantage in the ninth inning at Progressive Field, where a half-filled ballpark hoped to witness a fifth straight Tribe win. The polarizing pitcher surrendered a game-tying, solo home run to Dayan Viciedo on his third pitch. Three batters later, Alejandro De Aza took him deep to give Chicago the lead.

"We got the feeling of having the air taken out of us," infielder Mike Aviles recalled.

Jason Giambi approached the plate with two outs in the bottom of the ninth. Michael Brantley had singled and stolen second base. Giambi had tagged the White Sox for a walk-off home run two months earlier.

Giambi struck again.

On closer Addison Reed's third offering of the at-bat, Giambi socked a slider into the right-field seats to propel the Indians to a 5–4 victory. As soon as his bat struck the baseball, Giambi lifted the lumber high in the air with his right hand and flipped it aside. While his teammates crowded around home plate, anticipating the inevitable mob scene, Giambi slapped hands with third-base coach Brad Mills and spread his arms to brace himself for the celebratory drubbing. Jumping up and down, his teammates pounded him on the helmet and the backside and nearly yanked off his jersey.

"It's the stuff you dream about," Giambi said.

Shortstop Asdrubal Cabrera jumped into his arms. Jason Kipnis and Nick Swisher followed suit. Swisher and Mike Aviles doused him with Gatorade. Michael Bourn was lying on a table in the trainer's room after leaving the game with a wrist injury. As soon as Giambi's bat met ball, he leapt off the table and excitedly grabbed trainer Lonnie Soloff.

"I almost broke Lonnie's neck," Bourn said. "That was a big moment for us. We needed that game."

"I remember it like it was yesterday, just absolutely losing it," Aviles said.

"Coming down the stretch, trying to get a playoff berth," Giambi said, "it doesn't get any bigger than that. It really doesn't."

Giambi said he made Perez give him a hug, adding that the closer "was a little down" after blowing the lead. The 42-year-old became the oldest player in major league history to register a walk-off home run.

"None of us knew at that moment just how important it was," said team president Mark Shapiro. "When you look back, it was an incredible moment. For this to happen, for it to be a guy that our players felt that way about, just magnified what was already an unbelievable moment. Your range of emotions from Chris blowing the save to that happening, it was a pretty strong flop, just beyond belief."

The Indians forged ahead and won their remaining five games to clinch their first postseason berth since 2007. They capped the 10-game win streak—the longest such streak to end a regular season in franchise history—with a 5–1 victory at Target Field in Minnesota, as Twins outfielder Clete Thomas grounded out to second baseman Jason Kipnis to punch Cleveland's ticket to October baseball. Kipnis made a diving snag in the grass in short right field as pitcher Justin Masterson covered first, tagged the base and held the clinching baseball in his right hand, high above his head.

Jason Giambi celebrates the walk-off home run that propelled the Indians to a 5–4 victory over the Chicago White Sox on September 24, 2013.

Players, coaches and team executives sprayed each other with champagne in the clubhouse after the game, the franchise's first taste of celebratory bubbly in six years. The Indians amassed a 21–6 record in September. They finished the season with a 17–2 mark against the White Sox and a 13–6 record against the Twins. They closed the regular-season slate with six wins against those division foes, including a four-game sweep in the Twin Cities.

"Things were falling in place for us," Aviles said.

They fell short against the Rays in the Wild Card game, 4–0, before a boisterous sellout crowd of 43,579 in Cleveland. Still, the Indians reversed course in their first season under manager Terry Francona, as they leapt from 68 wins in 2012 to 92 in 2013.

Francona, who was named the American League Manager of the Year, frequently doled out credit to Giambi, who served as a veteran leader on a team devoid of much playoff experience. Francona first met Giambi two decades earlier when he was managing Double-A Birmingham and Giambi was playing at Double-A Huntsville. General manager Chris Antonetti said the club had "favorable reports" on Giambi's leadership, but could not have envisioned "the magnitude of his impact" until the team experienced it first-hand. Offseason additions of Swisher and Michael Bourn certainly contributed to a 21–6 September surge. However, Giambi's presence, Francona often quipped, was akin to having an extra coach on the roster. A coach who could also hit home runs, reliever Vinnie Pestano added.

Giambi batted just .183 with nine home runs in 186 at-bats for the Tribe in 2013, but following the Wild Card Game defeat, the Indians' first offseason transaction was to sign him to a minor

Fowl Ball

On September 4, 2013, the Indians made a call-up from their farm system. Pitcher Justin Masterson carried a live chicken to batting practice as a means of poking fun at reliever Cody Allen, nicknamed "Chicken Al," and to keep the Indians loose as they remained in the hunt for a Wild Card spot. The chicken pranced around the outfield grass as the pitchers shagged fly balls.

The Indians topped the Baltimore Orioles that evening, 6–4. They returned the bird to its coop after its one-time appearance at Progressive Field, but the Tribe rode the leftover magical vibes of the "Rally Chicken" to a playoff berth.

Under manager Terry Francona, the Indians have turned to fowl play when they need a spark. After an 0–6 West Coast road trip during the last week of April 2014, Masterson and fellow pitchers Scott Atchison and Corey Kluber sported bright yellow chicken costumes as they roamed the outfield during batting practice prior to the first game of the team's ensuing homestand. The Indians went 5–2 during the homestand.

league contract that included an invitation to spring training. Francona said the swift action taken on Giambi's status was no coincidence.

"I have so much, not just affection," Francona said, "but so much admiration for him."

31 The Dark Ages

From 1960 to 1993, the Indians finished better than fourth place just once—a third-place showing in 1968. They became the league punching bag, a perennial loser that played before sparse crowds at Cleveland Municipal Stadium.

So, when Gabe Paul took charge of the front office, he fixated on adding star power to the roster. It did not always work. In fact, it did not ever work.

"He tried to make a trade for a name that people could latch on to," said Bob DiBiasio, Indians senior vice president of public affairs, "whether it was Joe Carter, bringing Rocky Colavito back, getting Julio Franco, making blockbuster trades at the winter meetings, anything just to get people fired up and going."

It wasn't just Paul's follies, though. The Indians made a litany of poor signings and trades during the nearly four decades of dismal baseball.

After Wayne Garland posted a 20–7 record and 2.67 ERA for the Baltimore Orioles in 1976, the Indians signed the 26-year-old to a 10-year, $2.3 million contract. He could not believe a team valued him at that going rate, but he was not going to turn down the money. Garland went 13–19 with a 3.60 ERA and totaled 282⅔ innings in his first season with Cleveland. Then, he tore his rotator cuff. He won only 15 games over the next four seasons and the Indians released him after the 1981 campaign, halfway into his decade-long deal.

Dennis Eckersley won 14 games for the Indians as a 22-year-old in 1977. Then, the club traded him to the Boston Red Sox for Ted Cox (batted .224 with five home runs in two seasons with Cleveland), Bo Diaz (batted .254 with 12 home runs in four seasons with Cleveland), Mike Paxton (won 20 games with a 4.97 ERA in three seasons with Cleveland), and Rick Wise (lost a league-high 19 games in his first of two seasons with Cleveland). Eckersley won 20 games with Boston in 1978, when he finished fourth in balloting for the American League Cy Young Award. He went on to become one of baseball's most celebrated pitchers, excelling both as a starter and a closer.

Mired in Mediocrity

The Indians were an average or below-average team for nearly 35 years, with a few extremely miserable seasons mixed in. Here are the club's five best and five worst season records from the dark period of 1960-93.

Five best:
87–75, 1965 (fifth place)
86–75, 1968 (third place)
84–78, 1986 (fifth place)
81–78, 1976 (fourth place)
52–51, 1981 (sixth place)

Five worst:
57–105, 1991 (last place)
60–102, 1985 (last place)
60–102, 1971 (last place)
61–101, 1987 (last place)
62–99, 1969 (last place)

The team acquired hurler Gaylord Perry prior to the 1972 season. The spitballer captured the American League Cy Young Award in his first season in Cleveland. He spent three-plus years with the Tribe before the club dealt him to Texas. He was 36 years old at the time, but he proved he had plenty left in the tank. He tallied 63 wins over the next 3½ years and added more hardware to his mantle with the 1978 National League Cy Young Award. The three pitchers the Indians acquired in exchange for Perry combined for a 114–126 record during their tenures in Cleveland.

The Indians traded away 1971 American League Rookie of the Year Chris Chambliss in 1974. He blossomed into a cornerstone first baseman for the New York Yankees and Atlanta Braves. They dealt third baseman Graig Nettles to the Yankees in 1972. He was a steady force in New York's lineup for more than a decade, as he became a six-time All-Star. Following his trade to Texas in 1978, third baseman Buddy Bell won six Gold Glove awards and made four All-Star teams.

32 Meet Slider, Indians Mascot

As Carlos Baerga socked Bob Wells' offering into left field for a single, a strange creature hobbled along the warning track in right-center. Slider, the Indians' furry, fuchsia—umm, well, what species is he exactly?—mascot with a bushy yellow beak and eyebrows instantly gained nationwide recognition. During Game 4 of the 1995 American League Championship Series against the Seattle Mariners, the tubby critter tumbled off the outfield wall while dancing, plummeting to the field below.

Slider, the Indians' fuchsia-colored, furry mascot, dances on the dugout.
(AP Images)

"Meanwhile, the umpires don't see it. Slider is on the field," announcer Bob Costas said on the national telecast, expressing disbelief. "The mascot fell out of the stands and he is hobbling toward the bullpen."

Slider entered the open bullpen door and immediately dropped to the ground, writhing in pain in the bullpen dirt. It had been a rainy day in Cleveland and the top of the wall was slick. Slider, the Indians' mascot since 1990, fell victim to the conditions. Indians personnel, including relief pitcher Julian Tavarez, surrounded the character—and the man playing him, Dan Kilday, who actually did suffer injury.

"What if Baerga had hit a ball to right-center field?" Costas quipped. "The mascot is on the field and you've got a couple of outfielders converging on the ball. How bizarre would that have been?"

Kilday blew out his right knee, and when he returned to the costume the next day with a cast on his real leg, he added a pair of crutches and some bandages to Slider's get-up. He received a standing ovation when he entered Jacobs Field prior to Game 5.

Despite that snafu, Slider has been a steady face at Indians home games. He burst onto the scene at Cleveland Municipal Stadium, then a pink body in a sea of mostly empty seats. The team then shifted to Jacobs Field, it started winning and Slider became an integral part of the entertainment.

He became the fourth Major League Baseball mascot to be elected to the Mascot Hall of Fame when he was inducted on September 29, 2008, joining his counterparts the Phillie Phanatic, Mr. Met, and the San Diego Chicken.

33 Major League

Hank Peters, the Indians' president, called Bob DiBiasio into his office one afternoon in 1988. On Peters' desk sat the script to a potential movie, "Major League." Peters handed the document to DiBiasio, the team's public relations director, and said: "Here. For some reason, MLB is allowing Hollywood to do a movie on us. Here it is. Go for it. You're in charge."

DiBiasio had script approval. He presented the idea to the team.

"Our players had a lot of fun with it," DiBiasio said. "They loved it."

Some of the players, including knuckleballer Tom Candiotti, attended the premiere. Actors Charlie Sheen and Tom Berenger spent time with the club at Cleveland Municipal Stadium. Sheen and Mel Hall went out for a night in Cleveland.

"Who knows what *they* ended up doing," DiBiasio said.

The movie was officially released on April 7, 1989. Much of the film was actually shot in Milwaukee, but it was based on the woeful (both fictional and factual) Cleveland Indians, who needed a winning season to attract fans to the ballpark and prevent the team owner from relocating the franchise to Miami. A collection of goofy misfits starts the season off slowly, but bands together and makes a run at the American League pennant.

There is pitcher Ricky Vaughn, played by Sheen, who boasts a blazing fastball, but struggles to control it. There is outfielder Pedro Cerrano, played by Dennis Haysbert, who possesses a powerful swing, but is constantly overmatched by curveballs, so he tries voodoo to help his chances at the plate. There is third baseman Roger Dorn, played by Corbin Bernsen, a diva who is always concerned with his next contract. Catcher Jake Taylor, played by Berenger, has the knees of an 80-year-old and focuses on his ex-girlfriend. Hurler Eddie Harris, played by Chelcie Ross, has lost so much luster on his pitches that he resorts to doctoring the baseball. Center fielder Willie "Mays" Hayes, played by Wesley Snipes, flashes blistering speed on the base paths but can only hit pop-ups.

The group of oddballs ties the New York Yankees for first in the American League East, so the two clubs square off in a one-game playoff to decide the champion. Vaughn shuts down the Yankees in the top of the ninth with the score tied and Hayes scores from second on Taylor's bunt single in the bottom of the frame to win the game.

The movie grossed $50 million, debuted at No. 1 at the box office, and gave the real Indians their place in Hollywood lore.

34 Comedy of Errors

Omar Vizquel used to tell a lot of jokes. It was his way of keeping his team loose, though he contends he doesn't have what it takes to pursue a successful comedic career.

He did once perform a 20-minute standup routine at a club in the Flats in downtown Cleveland during All-Star week in 1997.

"I think it went pretty well," Vizquel said. "I didn't get booed or anything. They didn't throw tomatoes."

Vizquel's go-to joke goes something like this:

There was a football game pitting the world's large animals against the small animals. The team blessed with size dominated the first half of the affair. The large animals received possession of the ball to start the second half. On the first play, the elephant was stopped in his tracks. On the second play, the rhino was stopped in his tracks. On the third play, the hippo was stopped in his tracks. The small animals on defense huddled around the coach, who asked which player stopped the elephant. The centipede replied that he was responsible. The coach asked which player stopped the rhino. The centipede replied that he was responsible. The coach asked which player stopped the hippo. The centipede replied that he was responsible.

"Where were you during the first half?" the coach asked.

"Well, I was having my ankles taped."

Cue the laugh track … or something.

"Everybody's waiting for a punch line and then here it comes and we just bust out laughing," former pitcher Charles Nagy recalled. "We didn't know where this story was going and then the centipede was getting his ankle taped. I still use that joke. I tell my kids that joke."

Vizquel's teammates weren't laughing on April 16, 1994. This was no joke. The Indians' newest addition, playing in his ninth game with the team and known for his reputation as an elite defensive shortstop, made three errors.

"Nobody knew me in Cleveland," Vizquel said. "I made three errors in a game. Three errors."

Vizquel vividly remembers each miscue. He committed gaffes on consecutive plays in the top of the third inning. He missed a ground ball off the bat of Kansas City's Greg Gagne with one out. Two pitches later, Vince Coleman hit a grounder toward Vizquel, who corralled the baseball and, while attempting to initiate a double play, threw the ball away. Both runners were safe and proceeded to score later in the frame.

In the eighth, with the Indians unraveling and the bases loaded in a 9-9 game, Vizquel booted a pop fly. Two runs scored.

"Three errors," Vizquel repeated, almost amazed, years later, that he could have been responsible for such a litany of mistakes. "I remember a guy from the stands said, 'Send this guy back to Seattle!'"

It wasn't the ideal first impression to make on his new teammates.

"The first thing we said was, 'Who is this guy?'" said center fielder Kenny Lofton.

Vizquel didn't make another error until August 3, a span of 52 games. He committed six all season and earned his second consecutive Gold Glove Award. He would proceed to capture the honor for nine straight seasons—one with the Mariners and eight with the Indians. He tacked on two more to his collection later in his career with the San Francisco Giants.

"He made us a better defensive team," said second baseman Carlos Baerga. "I remember the first day he came up and he said to us, 'I watched you guys play the last few years and you guys make a lot of errors. For us to win, we need to play better defense.'"

Now, Vizquel, Lofton and the rest of the Indians can laugh at that shaky Saturday afternoon at Jacobs Field, a day in which pelting the shortstop with tomatoes might have been a warranted action.

35 Taking Back Tito

Terry Francona assisted with the Indians' scouting efforts in 2001. Whenever then-general manager Mark Shapiro asked Francona—who served as a special assistant that season—for his thoughts on a particular player, Francona steered him away. Ultimately, Shapiro asked Francona why he had not approved of any prospect.

"He said, 'You haven't said yes [to anyone],'" Francona said. "I figured the odds were in my favor if I said no. How do you know?"

Francona—whose father, Tito, played 15 years in the major leagues—was once a highly touted prospect himself. With the Tigers in 1959, Tito asked Detroit general manager John McHale for a $500 raise, extra income that would help support the son he and his wife, Roberta, were expecting. McHale scoffed at the notion, saying it wasn't his problem. The Tigers dealt Tito to the Indians that March. Terry was born a month later.

In 1980, the Expos selected Francona with the 22nd overall pick in the first-year player draft. Naturally, McHale happened to be Montreal's GM.

Tito said to McHale: "Do you remember that son that I wanted the $500 for?"

McHale remembered.

"Well, it's going to cost you a lot more now," Tito said, as both parties laughed.

A few days after he was drafted, Francona's University of Arizona team captured the college national championship. After the title game, Wildcats coach Jerry Kindall approached Francona, who had been named the Most Outstanding Player of the tournament, and told him it was time for him to move on to the next level.

"The only thing I was really stressed about," Francona said, "was I had done so horrible at class that semester that I was thinking, 'If I don't sign, I'm going to have to take summer school.'"

The Expos offered Francona a $100,000 signing bonus, which he accepted. Jim Fanning, Montreal's director of scouting, flew into town; Francona grew up in the small community of New Brighton, Pennsylvania. Tito and Roberta had Francona pick up Fanning from the airport and bring him back to the house. Roberta cooked a meal for everyone and they all chatted for a few hours. A week later, Francona officially joined the Expos organization.

He was almost a Chicago Cub. Before he ever attended college, Francona was drafted by the Cubs in the second round. They offered him an $18,000 signing bonus, but he was adamant about earning a $40,000 stipend.

Francona was well regarded. He panicked during his senior year of high school when his batting average "slipped" to .700. His stress level increased even more when he then separated his shoulder, which sidelined him for six weeks. He always dreamed of following in his father's footsteps. His seventh-period Spanish teacher often dismissed him from class early. He would drive his Mustang down to the baseball field and drag the dirt. When his effort did not finish the job, he would douse the field with four or five gallons of gasoline and light it on fire.

"I remember teachers saying, 'Damn, I thought the fucking building was burning,'" Francona said. "Nowadays, you'd probably go to jail. My Spanish teacher, she knew I didn't [care] about Spanish. I just wanted to play."

A handful of scouts flocked to New Brighton to watch him take batting practice off of his coach during his senior year. Longtime Cincinnati Reds scout Elmer Gray organized a showcase for Francona in which he performed a series of drills, including a pair of 60-yard dashes, two at-bats against a live pitcher, and a set of outfield throws.

When the Cubs refused to up their offer, however, Francona enrolled at Arizona. Then, as the clock wound down toward his first class, he became homesick and developed feelings of regret about turning down Chicago's proposal. Negotiations could continue until a player attended his first college class, so Tito checked back with the Cubs one final time to see if they would budge.

They did.

They offered Francona $19,000.

He went to class.

Those experiences provided Francona with plenty of insight that came in handy when he joined the Indians staff in 2001. Francona lasted parts of 10 seasons in the big leagues, as he compiled a .274 batting average with 16 home runs in 708 games. He hit .346 in 58 games for the Expos in 1984 before a knee injury marred his season. He never lived up to his billing as a first-round draft choice, and he said when he went out with Shapiro to scout in 2001, he "was humbled."

"You just never quite know," Francona said. "You see guys hit .350 in Triple-A and they get to the big leagues and if they have a hole—it may take the league [a while] to find it, but [they will]. There aren't a lot of guarantees."

Francona had more skill with communicating with players and practicing in-game strategy. He started managing the Philadelphia Phillies at the age of 37 in 1997. He led the Phillies for four years—all losing seasons, which included a pair of last-place finishes in the National League East—before he received a pink slip.

The Indians swooped in and hired him as a special assistant. He traveled with Shapiro to New Orleans to scout Tulane infielder Jake Gautreau and Louisiana State infielder Mike Fontenot. The Indians did not select either player. Francona sat in the team's draft room and observed. He spent time with the organization's minor league staff at each stop in the farm system. The Indians had an impending hole to fill in center field, as Kenny Lofton, then 35 years old, was bound to hit free agency. Francona evaluated seven or eight center fielders. Eventually, the club settled on a trade for 23-year-old Milton Bradley. Francona spent the year building a tight bond with Shapiro and his assistant, Chris Antonetti. Those relationships became the foundation for a reconnection later down the road.

The Indians sputtered to an abysmal 68–94 finish in 2012. A 5–24 showing in August derailed their faint postseason hopes. With six games remaining in the regular season, the club cut ties with manager Manny Acta. Bench coach Sandy Alomar Jr. served as interim skipper for the final week and he instantly became a finalist for the job. So, too, did Francona. It took one phone call from Shapiro and Antonetti and the man who directed the Red Sox to two World Series titles was interested in the opening. Francona said Cleveland was the only destination in which he desired to coach again, more than a year removed from an undesirable conclusion to his tenure in Boston. A 94-loss team hauled in a two-time world champion to infuse a winning attitude into its clubhouse.

"I don't think that we felt like it was definitively going to be some miracle cure," Shapiro said. "We felt like Terry was going to bring credibility and a change in culture and bring a huge injection of positive energy and he was going to bring experience."

Francona flourished in Boston, with a team stacked with quality veterans every year, thanks to the loaded pockets of the club's ownership. In Cleveland, he arrived into the opposite situation. That did not deter him from signing on.

"Chris was very honest about some of the challenges we may have, because I don't think he wanted me to come here and then be disappointed," Francona said. "I was so wanting to come here because of my relationships with those guys, that that far outweighs any of the challenges and when we have challenges, we seem to find a way to work through them together. I enjoy doing that."

His credibility helped the club lure free agents Nick Swisher and Michael Bourn to town. Immediately, the players in the clubhouse took a liking to their new commander. In Francona's first year, the Indians capped a 92-win regular season with a 10-game winning streak that catapulted the club into the playoffs. The Tribe hosted the American League Wild Card game, which it lost, 4–0. Still, it represented a 24-game turnaround. That year spent scouting prospects and networking in the organization, those experiences gained through the draft process—all of it paid off for both Francona and the Indians.

"We didn't really know exactly what we were," Shapiro said. "We wanted to hire the best guy possible who we trusted and respected and felt would make us better at our jobs and that would get the most out of our players and help make them better. It wasn't necessarily we brought him in to create a contender or we brought him in because we thought he could resuscitate those '11 and '12 years.

"It was just that he was the best guy."

36 Handsome Lou

Bob Feller referred to Lou Boudreau as the Indians' on-field leader, even as a 21-year-old shortstop in his rookie season. Feller also frequently commended his teammate for his boyish looks. Still, Boudreau, who played for the franchise from 1938–1950 and managed the team from 1942–1950, commanded the respect of a team littered with veterans. It was not always easy. Older players did not always give in. Eventually, though, Boudreau and the Indians were rewarded for their efforts. The kid from Illinois guided the team to a World Series title in 1948.

When the Indians made the 24-year-old Boudreau a player/manager prior to the 1942 season, they supported him with a staff of experienced coaches. That did not stop the skeptics. Other players had auditioned for the position and were less than pleased to learn a kid with only two full major league seasons under his belt received the job. Boudreau met resistance when making pitching changes. He was badmouthed by teammates. He helped assimilate Larry Doby, the first African American player in the American League, into the Indians' clubhouse, where not all teammates were accepting. He clashed with owner Bill Veeck. He was second-guessed by teammates, media and upper management. And he had to figure out how to balance his own responsibilities on the diamond with those that included overseeing the rest of the team.

The Indians were an average team under Boudreau from 1942–1947. Boudreau himself was an All-Star from 1940–1944 and again in 1947 and '48. He finished in the top 10 in balloting for American League Most Valuable Player in all but one season from 1940–1948. He led the league in doubles three times and in batting average once. He developed a reputation as one of the slickest fielding shortstops in baseball.

In 1948, the Indians battled with the New York Yankees and Boston Red Sox throughout the summer for American League supremacy. Cleveland fell four games off the pace in mid-September before rallying for 11 wins in 12 games to take a slight lead. Boudreau submitted the most productive season of his career. He batted .355 with a .453 on-base percentage, 34 doubles, 18 home runs, and 106 RBIs. He walked 98 times and struck out on only nine occasions. His efforts earned him the MVP award and the Indians topped the Red Sox in a one-game playoff to advance to the World Series against the Boston Braves, which Cleveland claimed in six games.

Boudreau played for and managed the Indians for two more years before wrapping up his career with the Red Sox. He ended his 15-year playing career with a .295 lifetime average. He racked up 1,162 wins as a manager, with a .487 winning percentage in 16 seasons in charge. He was inducted into the Baseball Hall of Fame in 1970.

Upon his induction, Commissioner Bowie Kuhn said: "There are hitters in the Hall of Fame with higher batting averages, but I do not believe there is in the Hall of Fame a baseball man who brought more use of intellect and advocation of mind to the game than Lou Boudreau."

37 The *SI* Jinx Strikes

Joe Carter's smile seemed natural. Cory Snyder's seemed more forced. The two sluggers stood in a makeshift batting stance, their pieces of lumber pointed toward the large Chief Wahoo logo hovering above them. "Indian Uprising," the *Sports Illustrated* cover read on April 6, 1987. "Believe it! Cleveland is the best team in the American League," the issue claimed. It pegged the Tribe for 94 wins and an American League pennant.

The Indians won 84 games under manager Pat Corrales in 1986, their highest win total in nearly two decades. They had guys who hit for average in Pat Tabler, Tony Bernazard, and Julio

Franco. They had a guy who hit for power in Cory Snyder. They had guys who hit for both average and power in Joe Carter, Brook Jacoby, and Mel Hall.

The offense performed up to expectations in 1987. Pitching is also important, though. Tom Candiotti, Phil Niekro, and Scott Bailes tied for the team lead in wins...with seven. Candiotti, a knuckleballer, finished with 18 losses and a 4.78 ERA. Niekro, a 48-year-old knuckleballer, posted a 5.89 ERA. Steve Carlton, an eventual Hall of Famer who was 42 at the time, fashioned a 5.37 ERA in 23 outings. Tribe pitching was a disaster. The team logged a 5.28 ERA and surrendered 957 runs.

On April 18, the Indians lost 16–3 to the Baltimore Orioles to fall to 1–10. Not even two full weeks into the regular-season slate, the club had fallen 10 games back in the American League East. By the end of the dismal season, the Indians, at 61–101, sat in the division cellar, 37 games out of first place.

Corrales was canned after the team took a 31–56 mark into the All-Star break. The team lost 33 games by five or more runs. It did not finish with a winning record in any month and in April, May, June, July, and September, it finished at least five games below .500.

It was not an Indian Uprising. The Indians were not the best team in the American League. Whether a result of the *Sports Illustrated* jinx or simply a severe miscalculation, the magazine cover did not prove clairvoyant. The Indians did not finish with a winning record again until 1994.

In late June 1987, *Sports Illustrated* ran a story titled “It Won’t Be An Indian Summer.” The author admitted that *SI*’s prognosticators were “maybe a tad off” in their projection on that year’s Cleveland squad.

38 K-Love

He was feisty on the diamond, always aggressive on the base paths, and undeterred in the outfield. He was feisty away from the field, never afraid to speak his mind or offer his opinion, even when unsolicited.

Kenny Lofton was a core piece of the Indians glory teams in the '90s. He was the table-setter at the top of the lineup, a speedy center fielder who regularly flashed his wheels. He was a part of the purge of personalities prior to the 1997 campaign, as the Tribe traded him to the Atlanta Braves for David Justice and Marquis Grissom. For one year, Lofton felt out of place. He had spent five statistically sound seasons with Cleveland. He did not hold a grudge, though. He understood the business. And after the Indians fell one scoreless frame shy of a World Series title in '97, he re-signed with the organization that gave him his chance to shine.

"Kenny didn't like being questioned about his abilities, about how he goes about dealing with himself," said Bob DiBiasio, Indians senior vice president of public affairs. "He was an honest, feisty guy."

His honesty was brutal, yet sometimes refreshing and commendable. In an era of increasing political correctness and vague speak, Lofton never buried his true beliefs. After closer Chris Perez challenged Tribe fans for not filling the seats of Progressive Field in 2012, Lofton objected and chimed in with a perspective about what it took to fuel 455 sellouts from 1995–2001. When the Indians qualified for the 2013 American League Wild Card Game, which they lost to the Tampa Bay Rays, Lofton contended that the Tribe had not truly made the playoffs. Lofton argued that a post-season series requires more than just one game. Nick Swisher took

"Can't Beat That"

Kenny Lofton points to a Sunday afternoon in early September 2000 as the best day of his career. He can accurately recite every numeral in his stat line from the 12–11 win against the Baltimore Orioles.

The speedy center fielder finished with four hits, four runs scored, and a franchise record-tying five stolen bases. He also won the game on a walk-off home run in the 13th inning.

"Can't beat that," Lofton said.

Lofton singled and stole second in the first inning. He scored on a Jim Thome single, as he tied the American League record with a run scored in 18 consecutive games. When the statistic was displayed on the scoreboard, fans lured him out of the dugout for a curtain call.

In the third inning, Lofton singled and stole both second and third. On his swipe of third, he scored on an errant pickoff throw by Baltimore catcher Brook Fordyce to first base. He notched a bunt single and stole second again in the fourth. He reached on a fielder's choice and swiped second in the seventh. He was intentionally walked in the 11th.

With one out in the 13th, he deposited a pitch from Mike Trombley into the visitor's bullpen. He kept the bat raised in his right arm as he watched the baseball soar over the fence.

"It was my second walk-off," Lofton said. "I was pretty proud of that."

issue with Lofton's comments and the two engaged in a face-to-face dispute about how to fairly measure the Indians' campaign.

The Indians were October regulars during Lofton's tenure in Cleveland. He was part of five of their six American League Central championships from 1995–2001. When he returned via midseason trade in 2007, he helped the team to a division crown for the first time since he departed six years earlier. With the Indians, Lofton made five American League All-Star teams. He led the league in stolen bases for five consecutive seasons and his 452 steals with the Tribe rank first in franchise history.

"In a sport of professional athletes, where they're all the best at what they do, he was head and shoulders above the rest in pure athleticism," said team president Mark Shapiro. "That athleticism, combined with his competitiveness, fueled incredible performance."

Lofton attended the University of Arizona on a basketball scholarship. He teamed with eventual NBA stars Steve Kerr and Sean Elliott in guiding the Wildcats to the Final Four in 1988 and the Sweet Sixteen a year later. During his junior year, Lofton tried out for Arizona's baseball team.

When he first joined the Houston Astros' farm system, he could not hit. Charlie Manuel, Lofton's hitting coach in the minors and majors with the Indians, taught him to "know thyself," and play to his strengths by utilizing his speed and instincts. By the time he stepped into the batter's box with the Indians, he wreaked havoc on opposing pitchers. He hit .310 or better each season from 1993–1997. He won four Gold Glove awards. He routinely scaled the center-field wall at Jacobs Field to rob the opposition of extra-base hits or home runs.

"He could be the most dynamic player in franchise history," DiBiasio said, "an incredibly skilled athlete who was able to take that skill and turn it into being a damn good baseball player."

Lofton knew he was talented. He knew his on-field production could be considered elite. That is what made his shortcomings on the Hall of Fame ballot so disheartening. Despite finishing his career with 2,428 hits, a .299 batting average, .372 on-base percentage, 622 steals and 1,528 runs, Lofton received only 18 votes on the 2013 ballot. He failed to garner the 5 percent of votes necessary to remain on the ballot another year.

"I really got penalized," Lofton said. "I felt like I wanted a chance for people to look at my numbers and look at what I did year after year after year. But now you get off the ballot your first year, it's like you're just kicked to the curb now."

Perhaps Lofton's name was overshadowed on the ballot by the presence of known users of performance-enhancing drugs. No player was elected in the 2013 class. Lofton admitted he wished he would have debuted on a different year's ballot, rather than one that included names such as Barry Bonds, Roger Clemens, Sammy Sosa, and Mark McGwire.

"The focus was not on myself and others," Lofton said. "It was only on whether they should put in cheaters."

In typical Lofton fashion, he was not shy about expressing his feelings on the topic.

"I can't be sour at the game per se," Lofton said. "I'm sour at the people who could have made certain decisions and didn't."

Nonetheless, Lofton remains one of Cleveland's most celebrated players. He was inducted into the Indians Hall of Fame in 2010.

"Kenny was a special player," said former teammate Sandy Alomar Jr. "He was an every-nighter, full of energy. He came ready to play every day."

39 Visit League Park

It originally opened its doors on May 1, 1891, a day in which Cy Young pitched the Cleveland Spiders to a 12–3 victory against the Cincinnati Reds. It hosted the Indians' only World Series-clinching win at home in 1920, the same year in which second baseman Bill Wambsganss registered the first Fall Classic unassisted triple play and Elmer Smith slugged the first Fall Classic grand slam. It served as the site for Babe Ruth's 500th home run, a towering shot to right field—a fence not far from home plate, but one that was tall, menacing, and not so easy to clear. It hosted the Cleveland Buckeyes of the Negro League, who won the organization's World Series in 1945.

League Park, home to the Indians from 1901–1946, played host to plenty of baseball history. It was where Addie Joss tossed his perfect game against the Chicago White Sox in 1908. It was where 17-year-old Bob Feller made his first major league start, a dazzling 15-strikeout performance against the St. Louis Browns.

The Indians, though, eventually moved to Cleveland Municipal Stadium, leaving behind the venue in an area that succumbed to socioeconomic hardship. The building itself deteriorated over time, becoming a shell of its former showy self. The Hough neighborhood, where it was situated, transitioned into a poverty-stricken community.

An article in *The Plain Dealer* on May 2, 1891, the day after the original debut of League Park, described it as "a magnificent opening in Cleveland—there never was one like it and there never may be again."

There was.

In August 2014, the city unveiled a refurbished League Park, at the same location, the corner of E. 66th Street and Lexington Avenue. The project, spearheaded for years by councilwoman Fannie M. Lewis, required $6.3 million in renovations. Artificial turf spans the field. A new building houses bathrooms and concessions and includes the park's original dugout steps. An original wall displays artwork of some of the legends who played at the stadium. There is a heritage museum and a statue of Lewis, who passed away before her vision was completed. In addition to serving as a beacon of Cleveland baseball history, the site hosts local teams' games and recreational contests.

On the afternoon of the grand re-opening, a sun-splashed summer day, former Indians sluggers Andre Thornton and Travis Hafner represented the franchise before a large gathering of fans and baseball heads. Hafner took part in a home run derby contest.

"Baseball is a game that spans generations and we are a city that has a historic franchise and that has had three stadiums," said team president Mark Shapiro. "To stand in the exact spot where the first professional and Major League Baseball was played in the city of Cleveland, to know that little kids will be able to play on this field that has been so incredibly restored and pristine in a neighborhood that I think will just really cherish it and take care of it—that historic link of baseball is just incredible."

40 Center of the Baseball Universe

A baseball icon, and former Indians slugger, tossed out the first pitch. Another Indians slugger swatted the most important pitch of the night to decide the entire event. The 1997 All-Star Game, played at Jacobs Field in the heart of downtown Cleveland in front of a sold-out crowd that had long desired the spotlight, showcased the best of Indians baseball.

It started with the annual Home Run Derby, an event won by Yankees slugger Tino Martinez. Tribe first baseman Jim Thome participated, but failed to swat any pitches over the fence.

Country singer LeAnn Rimes performed the National Anthem prior to the 68th edition of the Midsummer Classic. Earlier in the year, the 14-year-old won Grammy Awards for Best New Artist and Best Female Country Vocal Performance.

Five months earlier, Cleveland hosted the NBA All-Star Game at Gund Arena, next door to Jacobs Field. The Eastern Conference walked away victorious, as Cavaliers guard Terrell Brandon contributed 10 points and eight assists. Another hometown star helped his team in a national exhibition in the MLB contest.

But first, the game had plenty of antics. In the second inning, Mariners southpaw Randy Johnson sailed a pitch high above the head of Rockies slugger Larry Walker, who was known to fear the 6-foot-10 hurler. The baseball was so off the mark—and intentionally so—that it hit the backstop. Colorado's right fielder dropped to one knee, paused for a moment of contemplation as his life seemingly flashed before his eyes, stretched out his back, stood back up, flipped his helmet around backward, switched to the opposite side of the batter's box, and dug in to hit righty against the flamethrower. The sequence was reminiscent of a similar altercation between Johnson and Phillies first baseman John Kruk in the 1993 All-Star Game. After another fastball out of the zone—though not nearly as astray as the first offering—Walker retreated to the other side of the plate and flipped his helmet forward. He eventually drew a walk.

The American League grabbed a 1–0 lead in the second inning when Seattle's Edgar Martinez clubbed a leadoff home run

Midwestern Hospitality

The Indians hosted the 1981 All-Star Game at Cleveland Stadium on August 9. The exhibition had been pushed back because of a players' strike, which forced the cancellation of nearly two months of the season.

Len Barker, the Indians' ace, had compiled a 5–3 record and 2.08 ERA prior to the All-Star break. He tallied seven complete games (including two shutouts) in his 10 starts. On May 15, Barker threw the eighth perfect game in Major League Baseball's modern era. He blanked the Blue Jays in a 3–0 win and registered 11 strikeouts.

Given Barker's early-season success, the Indians believed the right-hander deserved to start for the American League in front of his home crowd. Instead, Detroit's Jack Morris, who posted a 9–3 record and 2.56 ERA in 13 first-half starts, was tabbed to take the mound first. Morris tossed a pair of scoreless innings, as he limited the National League to two hits and one walk. Barker then took over and retired all six batters he faced. Pete Rose, Dave Concepcion, Dave Parker, Mike Schmidt, George Foster, and Andre Dawson—who combined for 58 career All-Star Game appearances—all made outs against Barker.

off of Braves right-hander Greg Maddux. The National League responded in the top of the seventh, as Atlanta catcher Javy Lopez deposited a pitch from Kansas City lefty Jose Rosado over the wall. Then, the hometown hero was anointed.

Yankees outfielder Bernie Williams drew a one-out walk in the seventh and advanced to second on a wild pitch with two outs. Indians catcher Sandy Alomar Jr. then struck a pitch over the outside part of the plate from San Francisco hurler Shawn Estes. The ball landed in the left-field bleachers as the Jacobs Field crowd went into a frenzy. The two-run shot provided the American League with a 3–1 advantage, one it would not relinquish. New York closer Mariano Rivera shut the door in the ninth inning, as Florida's Moises Alou lined out to Minnesota second baseman Chuck Knoblauch to end the game.

Cleveland has hosted the All-Star Game on five occasions: 1935, 1954, 1963, 1981, and 1997. After the '97 affair, Alomar delivered a message to Tribe fans.

"They've been hungry for this situation, for the All-Star Game," Alomar said on the national broadcast. "They've been talking about this the whole year. This is a gift from God. The whole year, they've been outstanding."

41 Stick a Cork in It

Few pitchers are recognized more for a covert operation than for a complete game. Few pitchers are known because of their stealthy ways and not their four-seam fastball. Jason Grimsley is not a household name for bouncing around the league for nearly two decades or for winning 42 games or for leading the league in hit-by-pitches in 1996. Any familiarity with his name likely stems from his participation in one of baseball's most bizarre tales.

Albert Belle corked his bats. His teammates knew it. Opponents thought it. White Sox manager Gene Lamont was tipped off to it before a game on July 15, 1994, at Comiskey Park. So in the first inning of the tilt between the top two teams in the American League Central, Lamont approached umpire Dave Phillips and disputed the legality of Belle's lumber. Phillips stored the bat in his locker in the umpires' dressing room. Grimsley had to make his move. The pitcher had the night off anyway, so why not set out on an adventure?

Grimsley retreated to the clubhouse to survey the scene and plot out his route to the umpires' room to replace Belle's bat. He described the deed as a puzzle. He stepped up onto the desk in the office of manager Mike Hargrove, removed a ceiling tile and lifted himself up into a narrow passageway. Grimsley brought a flashlight and an uncorked bat from teammate Paul Sorrento. Why not replace Belle's bat with another one of Belle's bats? All of his lumber was corked, as Omar Vizquel would attest eight years later in his autobiography.

At one point along his dark travels, Grimsley removed a ceiling tile for what he believed was the umpires' room. It was not. A groundskeeper sat on a couch below. Grimsley tried again. His heart racing, he removed another tile. This time, he was correct. Had anyone entered the room, Grimsley would have been in serious trouble. The door to the room had been locked and the bat was somewhat shielded in Phillips' locker. Grimsley descended onto the top of a refrigerator and lowered himself to the ground. He identified Belle's bat and switched it with Sorrento's used model, which bore the name of the first baseman. The swap could not have been more obvious. Grimsley re-entered the ceiling, made his way back to the Indians' clubhouse and spread the word with his teammates that the bats had been switched.

Upon the conclusion of the game, a 3–2 Tribe victory, the umpires quickly noticed the misconduct. Phillips was certain someone had broken in. White Sox owner Jerry Reinsdorf referred to the exchange as a "serious crime." Commissioner Bud Selig asserted that the league, which immediately launched an investigation, would "get to the bottom of this."

The league eventually worked out an agreement with the Indians. The intruder would not be sentenced if the team provided Belle's original bat to the American League office. The Tribe complied. Belle received a 10-game suspension, which, after an appeal, was whittled down to seven games. Grimsley's identity remained a secret until he revealed his journey through the bowels of the ballpark some five years later.

"Those little controversies are fun," said Bob DiBiasio, Indians senior vice president of public affairs. "It doesn't mean a whole lot. It wasn't like he was the only guy corking a bat. It's been happening in baseball forever and ever."

42 The End of an Era

Mark Shapiro knew months in advance that he would be taking over as the Indians' general manager in November 2001. He also knew that his reign as the team's chief roster decision-maker would likely begin with some unpopular choices, ones that signaled an end to the franchise's most successful era, ones he felt were necessary if the organization was to ever again reach a similar standard.

Shapiro informed his bosses, owner Larry Dolan and his son, Paul, the team president, that a shift in strategy was required. He warned them of the impending seismic transition. The Indians' near-decade of talent accumulation—executed through spending on the free-agent market and trading minor league prospects for proven performers—left the farm system barren.

"I couldn't necessarily chart a clear path back," Shapiro said.

A month after his promotion to the GM position became official, the Indians traded perennial All-Star second baseman Roberto Alomar to the Mets. In return, the Tribe acquired prospects Alex Escobar, Billy Traber, and Earl Snyder; pitcher Jerrod Riggan, and veteran outfielder Matt Lawton. Six days later, as an accompanying move, the club signed 31-year-old infielder Ricky Gutierrez to a multi-year contract to replace Alomar. Those transactions, to Shapiro, weren't completed with enough commitment. If the Indians were going to dive head-first into a rebuilding plan, they needed to part with veterans and stockpile promising young talent.

"That was a flawed execution because it was in the middle," Shapiro said.

He corrected that so-called "flawed execution" with a heist of the Montreal Expos in an exchange that included ace pitcher Bartolo Colon.

"Colon was kind of the flip of the switch," Shapiro said, "like, 'Hey, we have to be on.'"

The Indians dealt Colon and fellow right-handed hurler Tim Drew for veteran first baseman Lee Stevens and three minor league prospects: center fielder Grady Sizemore, left-handed pitcher Cliff Lee, and second baseman Brandon Phillips.

Shapiro remembers the exact date of the swap: June 27, 2002.

"Think about how early that is," Shapiro said.

There are reasons the Indians dashed to the front of the transaction line more than a month before the non-waiver trade deadline. The Indians were desperate, in need of organizational replenishing. The Expos were more desperate, in jeopardy of being contracted. Montreal GM Omar Minaya eventually became a close friend of Shapiro's, but in 2002, he had not been on the job very long. Thus, he did not have extensive knowledge of the Expos' minor league system. Meanwhile, the Indians employed Montreal's former farm director. Minaya was tasked with improving his big league club in order to make a run at the postseason, attract more fans to Olympic Stadium, and attempt to stave off contraction.

"He was highly motivated with the short-term horizon," Shapiro said. "We knew that. That's why we made the trade on June 27 instead of waiting."

Sizemore was a 19-year-old outfielder whom the Expos had selected in the third round of the amateur draft two summers earlier. The teenager did not display much power at the Expos' lower ranks, as he clubbed only three home runs in 253 games in their organization. He did demonstrate patience at the plate and an ability to reach base consistently, rare traits for such an inexperienced kid. He posted a .380 on-base percentage as a 17-year-old in the rookie league and a .381 on-base percentage the following year at Class A Clinton. When he joined the Indians' organization, the power arrived as well. Sizemore earned his way onto three American League All-Star teams while with the Tribe. He totaled at least 22 home runs, 76 RBIs, 22 stolen bases, 34 doubles, and 101 runs scored in each season from 2005–2008. He won a pair of Gold Glove awards and finished in the top 12 in American League Most Valuable Player balloting on three occasions. He tallied a league-high 53 doubles and 134 runs scored in 2006.

Lee, then a 23-year-old southpaw, was a fourth-round draft choice in 2000. He made his big league debut for the Tribe in 2002, posting a 1.74 ERA in two starts. He proceeded to win 46 games for the Indians from 2004–2006 and captured the American League Cy Young Award with a 22–3 record and 2.54 ERA in 2008.

Phillips spent his 21st birthday on June 28, 2002, packing his bags for Buffalo, New York, the site of the Indians' Triple-A affiliate. Montreal's second-round draft pick in 1999, the middle infielder had already established himself as one of the league's premier prospects. He burst onto the big league scene that season, though he never attained solid footing with the Tribe. He bounced between Buffalo and Cleveland until the start of the 2006 campaign, when the Indians dealt him to Cincinnati, where he flourished.

All three stars had unceremonious exits from Cleveland. Injuries derailed Sizemore's career. The Tribe traded Lee amid yet another rebuilding process in 2009. Phillips sparred with manager Eric Wedge and was exiled to Cincinnati in a lopsided exchange that left Cleveland with reliever Jeff Stevens. Still, the Colon trade is one of the more one-sided executions in league history. It allowed the Indians to jump-start their roster transformation.

"Is there any way to do it non-traditionally? Traditionally is eight, nine, 10 years," Shapiro said. "You lose enough to pick at the top and those guys get to the big leagues and you do that for three or four years. It takes a long time for that to happen.

"We decided we wanted to expedite that, because this place had been used to winning for a long time. So, Colon represented that rare opportunity to infuse three top-level talents into our farm system and do it at the upper levels where you sped up that timeframe."

Cleveland hit rock bottom in 2003, when the Indians amassed a 68–94 record, but they won at least 78 games each season from 2004–2008, including 93 in '05 and a league-high 96 in '07. The stretch did not quite resemble the one from the '90s—the ballpark wasn't sold out every night and they didn't field a team of household names and All-Stars—but it was a start.

"I don't think any of us realized how incredible an achievement it would be to turn an entire team over and get back to 93 wins in three years," Shapiro said. "When you look back at that, that was pretty good. But at that point, you're saying, 'Anything is possible. We can do that.'"

43 The First Taste of Victory

The fate of the 1920 World Series may have changed once Elmer Smith took a powerful hack in the first inning of Game 5. Charlie Jamieson, Bill Wambsganss, and Tris Speaker had all singled to load the bases. Smith then uncorked the first-ever World Series grand slam over the right-field fence at League Park, referred to at the time as Dunn Field.

Suddenly the Indians, who had trailed 2–1 in the series to the Brooklyn Robins, had a comfortable lead and the inside track at a 3–2 series advantage. The Indians forged ahead for an 8–1 victory in Game 5, a contest that oozed with baseball lore. In addition to Smith's feat, Wambsganss etched his name into the sport's history books.

Wambsganss snagged a line drive off the bat of Brooklyn pitcher Clarence Mitchell in the fifth inning. The runners on first and second base had taken off for their next destination, allowing Wambsganss to complete an unassisted triple play, the second ever recorded and the first in the postseason.

Jim Bagby, who set a franchise record with 31 wins during the regular season, pitched nine innings for the win and contributed a three-run home run. The Indians blanked Brooklyn in Games 6 and 7. Duster Mails tossed a three-hit shutout in Game 6 and Stan Coveleski clinched the series with a five-hit shutout in Game 7.

The Cleveland Press displayed a headline of "All Over—We win" with a subhead of "Atta boy, Tris" (a commendation of player/manager Speaker) in the following day's newspaper. A crowd of 200,000 lined Euclid Avenue to applaud the team in a victory parade.

Speaker once quipped: "The American boy starts swinging a bat about as soon as he can lift one." He would know. He burst onto the big-league scene as a 19-year-old in 1907. He batted .388 for the Indians in 1920 and, during the World Series, he hit .320 and scored six runs.

Some say it may never have happened if not for the Black Sox Scandal. Chicago—in contention with Cleveland for the American League pennant—had three games to play in 1920 when it was revealed that eight players had thrown the 1919 World Series, which the White Sox dropped to the Cincinnati Reds. The seven players still remaining on the team were suspended for the final three games in 1920. The White Sox lost two of the three and the Indians finished with a two-game cushion in the standings at the end of the regular season.

44 Wild Wednesday

Indians fans grew spoiled. Every October, a sellout crowd filed into the ballpark to watch the drama, the duress, and the desperation that come with postseason baseball. The Indians were regular participants from 1995-2001.

It became easy to get used to. It became the standard. It became possible to lose sight of how difficult it was to reach that point. Radio play-by-play announcer Tom Hamilton started calling Indians games in 1990. He considers himself lucky for suffering through four years of losing baseball in Cleveland before the Tribe reversed course and started winning. He said he acquired an appreciation for how difficult it is to achieve sustained success.

Nothing lasts forever, though. After an early exit in 2001, the Indians didn't qualify for the postseason again until 2007. When you grow accustomed to something and it suddenly eludes you, it can be difficult to cope. There's an unfamiliar emptiness, an unexpected void.

"I look back at it now and I still didn't appreciate it," Hamilton said. "When you're going through it, you're like, 'This will happen forever. These guys will never get old and we'll go to the World Series every year.'"

It does, however, make the more sporadic triumphs even sweeter. After coming within one win of a trip to the Fall Classic in 2007, the Indians endured another rebuilding phase that saw the organization trade away Cy Young Award winners in CC Sabathia and Cliff Lee. The club tallied 93 or more losses in 2009, 2010, and 2012. There was a mass exodus of players from that 2007 playoff team. Eric Wedge was canned and then Manny Acta came and went as manager. Everything changed in 2013, when the Tribe, one year removed from a 94-loss season that included an abysmal 5–24 showing in August, accelerated their comeuppance.

Their first taste of playoff baseball in six years lasted less than four hours, but those cherished minutes provided the championship-starved city with another reminder of the distinctiveness of October baseball. The ballpark was electric. The city was alive and tangibly buzzing.

"That vibe that night was just absolutely incredible," said Jim Thome, the club's all-time leader in home runs.

The Indians called upon a 23-year-old kid with 10 major league starts to his name to toe the rubber before the raucous 43,579 fans who squeezed into Progressive Field. When the Indians clinched a Wild Card Game berth on the final Sunday of the regular season, manager Terry Francona informed rookie hurler Danny Salazar that he would take the hill three days later with the club's postseason fate hanging in the balance. The Dominican Republic native became the third-youngest hurler in franchise history to start a playoff game.

It wasn't Salazar's first bout with pressure. In July, he tossed and turned the night before his big league debut, so much so that he fell back asleep after his alarm clock went off in the morning. He ultimately woke in a panic, dashed to the ballpark, and arrived at the Indians' clubhouse less than an hour before his scheduled first pitch. He proceeded to carry a no-hitter into the sixth inning against the Blue Jays. He departed his debut after six frames, in which he limited Toronto to one run on two hits and a walk. He struck out seven.

Salazar was nervous and jittery only up until he resided upon his most comfortable setting.

"I asked him after his first start: 'How nervous were you?'" Francona said. "He was like, 'Not really.' And usually you get that from guys and you know they're lying. He explained it to me that, 'I've been through so much with my arm, being on the mound is the most comfortable place for me in the world.'"

After that outing, Salazar returned to Triple-A. The Indians summoned him again in early August, and the right-hander remained in the team's starting rotation for the duration. He posted a 3.12 ERA in his 10 starts, a welcome boost to an injury-riddled group.

So, on that Wednesday evening, Salazar stood atop the mound, with a house full of red-shirt-wearing, white-towel-waving backers howling at his near-untouchable heater. Fellow pitcher Joe Smith called the pitch a "lightning fastball." Salazar admitted to having a small dose of nerves at the start of the contest, but that only amped up his velocity. He capped a scoreless first inning when he blew away Tampa Bay's James Loney with a 100-mph fastball.

After Salazar set down the Rays in order in each of the first two frames, Delmon Young swiftly silenced the crowd with a solo home run into the left-field bleachers to start the third. Desmond

Jennings then plated a pair of runs with a two-out double to left in the fourth. The Indians out-hit the Rays nine to eight in the contest, but Cleveland stranded nine runners and went 2-for-9 with runners in scoring position. Tampa Bay righty Alex Cobb scattered eight hits over 6⅔ scoreless innings. Salazar departed early in the fifth inning, having surrendered three runs on four hits.

The Indians could not muster a timely hit. The bats went dormant at the most critical junctures. The Tribe fell short, 4–0, as the Rays advanced to the American League Division Series against the Red Sox. Cleveland's October experience was short-lived. A tease, almost.

Still, the three hours—and the buildup the three days before it—served as a reminder of the magic of the postseason. No, it's no longer an annual guarantee. But every trip to October is still some sort of sweet.

"Those moments, when you see this place like that and you look down and you see the parents and grandparents in the stands and the little kids, you're thinking, 'This building is multi-generational now,'" said team president Mark Shapiro. "There are people who came here as little kids who are now here with their kids and have talked about what it was like to be here in the mid-'90s and now they're saying, 'This is what it was like.' You do these jobs to see that and feel that and know that you're impacting families and kids that way."

45 Cleveland Municipal Stadium

Cleveland Stadium played host to the Indians' home games for nearly 60 years through the 1993 season. For much of that time period, it also served as the Cleveland Browns' home. When the Indians played, the diamond still showed signs of a football field, so much so that on a lazy fly ball, center fielder Rick Manning would raise his hand to signal for a fair catch.

Bob DiBiasio, the Indians' senior vice president of public affairs, once went for a run around the field on a Monday afternoon. The Indians had a home game that evening. The Browns had played there the previous day. As DiBiasio jogged around the track, he noticed the orange helmet logo still painted between the pitcher's mound and second base. DiBiasio sprinted back upstairs to the front offices, where he found team president Gabe Paul. DiBiasio begged his boss to venture outside and take a look at the field. It would not be the best look for the Indians to play on an orange infield with the logo of a team from a different sport.

Paul was angry. He yelled...at DiBiasio, for breaking the dress code by wearing gym shorts and a sweat-covered T-shirt around the office.

Ultimately, Paul agreed to see the field and he became even more livid upon seeing the Browns logo. So, the grounds crew cut a square at the location of the logo, removed it and re-sodded it. By the time first pitch rolled around, viewers could notice the patchwork fix, but at least infielders were not blinded by vibrant orange grass on ground balls.

Such was life for the Indians, who were just a tenant in a massive building they shared for decades. They played their first game at the venue on July 31, 1932, when hurler Mel Harder toed

A Hope and a Prayer

After the final out of the 1993 season—the last ever recorded at Cleveland Stadium—Bob Hope sang a version of the song "Thanks for the Memory" on the field. The tune was filled with lyrics specifically written about the ballpark. Bob DiBiasio escorted the 90-year-old and his wife, Dolores, to the pitcher's mound, where Hope addressed the crowd.

Prior to the performance, DiBiasio had asked the longtime actor, singer, and comedian if he needed a podium upon which he could place his script. That way, in case he clutched the microphone in his hand, he would have a free hand to turn the pages.

Hope responded: "Young man, I've been doing vaudeville since I was 15 years old. I've never touched a microphone in my life."

As soon as Hope positioned himself in front of the mound, he grabbed the microphone from its stand. He held the mic in his right hand and his script in his left hand. When he needed to turn the page, he wouldn't be singing into the mic. DiBiasio described it as "a mess."

"All you heard was people going, 'We couldn't hear him!'" DiBiasio said.

He turned to Dolores and said, "We need to get that mic back into the mic stand."

She leaned over and replied: "You're on your own, kid."

And thus, Cleveland Stadium was laid to rest.

the rubber. Then, however, the team still played most of its games at League Park. The Indians truly transitioned to the shores of Lake Erie in the 1940s.

When the place was filled to capacity, it provided an overwhelmingly energized atmosphere. That did not happen often. For much of its existence, the cavernous building remained mostly deserted, as struggling teams played before, relatively speaking, a handful of fans. During its lifespan, it seated between 73,000–79,000 for baseball games. For that debut in 1932, it attracted 80,184, then a major league record. Gradually, the Tribe played more and more games at Cleveland Stadium. First, it was only Sunday and holiday affairs. Then, they shifted the important matchups to the larger stadium. When the league implemented night games into the schedule, the Indians shifted there when the sun went down, since League Park lacked lights. Once the 1940 campaign rolled around, the team played the vast majority of its schedule on the waterfront. It removed League Park from its plans after the 1946 season.

Because it also hosted football games, the outfield was vast and spacious. The stands were far removed from the field, so fans—when they showed up—were not as involved in the action. Its proximity to Lake Erie enticed swarms of pesky insects. Cleveland Stadium played host to four All-Star games (1935, 1954, 1963, 1981); a World Series championship in 1948; Ted Williams' 500th home run (June 17, 1960); Ten Cent Beer Night (June 4, 1974); and Len Barker's perfect game (May 15, 1981). It closed its doors to baseball on October 3, 1993, and remained the home of Browns football for two more years.

46 Snow-pening Day

In 2007, Milwaukee's Miller Park played host to the Indians' "home" opener. The Tribe had Mother Nature to thank for that.

An early-April snowstorm wiped out a four-game set against the Mariners that was intended to take place at Jacobs Field. The record books display no evidence of competition at Cleveland's ballpark that weekend, but the Indians were actually one out away from notching a victory—not to mention a truncated no-hitter.

The Indians and Mariners endured a light but steady snowfall as they braved the Friday afternoon conditions. Cleveland staked claim to a 4–0 lead before Mariners manager Mike Hargrove—nicknamed "The Human Rain Delay" during his playing days for his lengthy, time-stalling at-bat rituals—griped that his batter, Jose Lopez, could not see the baseball through the falling flakes. Umpire Rick Reed opted to delay the game, but Mother Nature never relented. Eventually, the game was called and Indians hurler Paul Byrd's 4⅔ innings of no-hit baseball went out the window.

The game was initially rescheduled as part of a split double header the following day, but the snow did not cease. Weather wiped out the entire series and forced the Indians to relocate to Milwaukee, where they hosted a three-game set against the Angels. The Brewers sold tickets to each contest for $10 apiece and the series attracted more than 52,000 fans.

Slider, the Indians' mascot, made the trip. So, too, did drummer John Adams, who has banged on his 26-inch bass drum at nearly every Indians home game since 1973. Adams received a

Snow Days

For two years, Progressive Field morphed into a winter wonderland. From late November into January, the Indians filled the ballpark with the constructions required to host cold-weather activities.

Atop the left-field bleachers sat the Batterhorn, a 10-lane snow tubing hill. Along the outfield warning track rested an ice skating path dubbed the Frozen Mile. A small ice skating rink was tucked away in the left-field corner near Slider's Snow Mountain, a kids' play area. They placed a fire pit on the home run porch and a walking trail with winter lights through the outfield. They hosted hockey games on the Frozen Diamond. On January 15, 2012, the ballpark hosted a hockey game between Ohio State University and the University of Michigan. The matchup, the first-ever outdoor college hockey game in the state, was dubbed The Frozen Diamond Face Off.

The Indians hosted the winter event in 2010–11 and 2011–12, but ceased production after two years because of low attendance.

The words "Welcome to Opening Day 2007" conjure images of a sunny April day, but in fact the Jacobs Field Opening Day game against the Mariners had to be called due to a snowstorm.

call from a woman in the Indians' front office on Monday, April 9. She asked if Adams could travel to Milwaukee on Tuesday.

Adams replied: "No. There's a baseball game. I can't go to Milwaukee."

"She goes, 'Oh, you haven't heard?'" Adams said. "'We've decided, because of the snow, we're going to play the series with the Angels in Milwaukee.'"

Adams reached out to his boss at his day job at a local phone company and got people to take on his work shifts for the following three days. He called back the Indians employee and committed to drumming at the series at Miller Park. Adams needed a case to tote his drum north. He met a man halfway and picked up a 28-inch case that protected his old instrument.

The Indians claimed two of three games from the Angels. In the rubber match, Travis Hafner slugged a game-winning, three-run home run in the eighth inning to erase a 2–1 deficit. The club returned to Cleveland and hosted the White Sox at Progressive Field on Friday, April 13, a week after its originally scheduled home opener.

To make up the four games with the Mariners, Seattle traveled to Cleveland to play games on May 21, June 11, and August 30. Due to logistical challenges, the teams made up the fourth tilt at Safeco Field in Seattle as part of a twin bill lodged in the center of a four-game series in late September. In the first game, the Indians served as the home team and batted last. In the nightcap, the Mariners returned to their role as the home team in their home ballpark.

"You knew in the back of your mind that this was going to create a challenge for us," said team president Mark Shapiro, then the club's general manager. "We were going to end up having to play a lot of games in a row. We were going to lose a lot of off days. We just lost a home series. In the end, what became apparent was that that team was not going to accept that. They weren't going to take the excuses. They were just good from day one on and defied the odds."

47 Visit the Player Statues

Perhaps one day, alongside the bronze likenesses of Jim Thome and Bob Feller, will stand a statue of Albert Belle in an intimidating pose, his finger pointing to his flexing bicep as he offers a menacing glare. That statue would probably come best as a package deal with one of former pitcher Jason Grimsley crawling on all fours, as he did to retrieve Belle's corked bat from a locked room in

Lineup Exchange

Progressive Field was filled with nostalgia on September 22, 2011. Before the first pitch between the Indians and White Sox, Jim Thome—Cleveland's 41-year-old designated hitter—and Omar Vizquel—Chicago's 44-year-old utility infielder—exchanged lineup cards.

The two spent nine years as teammates with the Indians. They accounted for eight All-Star appearances, 11 Gold Glove awards (all won by Vizquel), and more than 5,000 hits.

"They've accomplished a lot of things that many other players haven't accomplished," said their former teammate, Sandy Alomar Jr.

Both Thome and Vizquel played one more year in the big leagues, but neither with the Indians. This was the last time the two exchanged pleasantries in Cleveland while still active players.

"To be able to still play and to be able to take the lineup card and have him do it as well," Thome said, "is very special, especially here in Cleveland, where we played during the golden years of our careers. To have fun with that is great."

Comiskey Park in Chicago in 1994. Perhaps they could be joined by a statue of Fausto Carmona, as he was then named, standing atop the mound, his glove in front of his face, midges crawling up and down his skin as he resists the temptation to submit to their pestering ways. Or what about a model of former closer Chris Perez, waving his hand in front of his face to tell the opposition that they cannot see him, as he once did to Kansas City outfielder Jarrod Dyson while completing a save? How about a statue of Jose Canseco rubbing his noggin? Canseco never played for the Indians, but Cleveland Stadium was the site in which Carlos Martinez's fly ball bounced off of his dome and over the fence for a home run.

For years, a statue of Feller, rocking back in his windup with his front leg extended high in the air, stood alone outside of Progressive Field. The Indians unveiled one of Thome, in his patented stance with his bat pointed out into the abyss, on August 2, 2014. His

Indians fans admire the statue of Hall of Fame pitcher Bob Feller outside Progressive Field.

lumber is wrapped with tape. His helmet is slapped with pine tar. Thome appreciates the intricacies.

"I love it. I absolutely love it," he said. "You don't really ever think of getting a statue at all. It's humbling, it's honoring, and it's something I think my family will live every day the rest of their lives."

A Larry Doby statue will join the two in 2015 and the Indians plan to build more as time elapses. The statues offer a glimpse into the history of the franchise, as they stand tall above anyone who ventures to look at them.

"I don't think anyone could be comfortable getting a statue, and I mean that respectfully," Thome said. "You play the game as a kid, you progress and go to high school, you get drafted and you go through the minor leagues. Nobody ever dreams of a statue. I certainly didn't."

48 The Quest for 200

Carlos Baerga and Sandy Alomar Jr. argued back and forth during a moment of reminiscing.

"Three days," Alomar said. "Not a week."

"A week!" Baerga insisted.

"Three days."

"A week."

"I have to refresh your memory," Alomar said.

To Baerga, the memory is crystal clear. It is one of a few that stands out the most in his major league career. Baerga was stuck on 199 hits for the season in 1993. More pertinent, he was stuck in a hospital bed with an infection in his leg, acquired after fouling a ball off of his ankle with about a week remaining in the regular season. Baerga begged his way out of the hospital and back onto the field for Game 160, the first contest of the Tribe's final series at Cleveland Stadium.

Mike Hargrove slotted Baerga into his usual No. 3 spot in the batting order. The second baseman—who served as the designated hitter that night—went hitless in his first three at-bats. In his fourth and final trip to the plate, he noticed the White Sox third baseman was playing back, so, with runners on first and second, he dropped a bunt down the baseline. Baerga sprinted down the line, safely crossed first base, and dropped to the ground in pain.

"The thing about Carlos," said former teammate Kenny Lofton, "we always talk about why Carlos ran so slow. He swears he runs fast. When you run, you go forward. Carlos is the only guy in major league history that runs and he goes sideways."

No matter his running style, Baerga had enough speed on his gimpy limb to leg out his 200th hit. It marked the second consecutive year he reached that plateau. Granted, he had to return to the hospital and did not play again that season.

"I had to get 200 hits," Baerga said.

Baerga earned three trips to the All-Star Game during his tenure with the Indians. He contributed to one of the league's most potent offenses. He batted .312 with 20 home runs and 105 RBIs in 1992. He followed that up with a .321 average, 21 home runs, and 114 RBIs in 1993. He became the first player at his position with consecutive seasons of 200 hits, 20 home runs, 100 RBIs, and a .300 batting average since Rogers Hornsby seven decades earlier. Baerga hit .314 in each of the next two seasons until Cleveland traded him during the 1996 campaign. The Indians cycled through second basemen for three years before luring Roberto Alomar to the lakeshore.

The 200-hit story—no matter how much Baerga exaggerates it or his teammates downplay it—is one of which he is quite proud. So, too, is he about a couple of other feats he accomplished.

On April 8, 1993, Baerga became the first player in big league history to slug a home run from both sides of the plate in the same inning. He tagged New York Yankees hurlers Steve Howe and Steve Farr during a nine-run seventh at Municipal Stadium. In a 9–5 loss to the Detroit Tigers at Tiger Stadium on June 17, 1993, Baerga socked a career-high three home runs, all off Detroit right-hander Mike Moore. Baerga drove in all five Cleveland runs that afternoon.

"That was a day that I'm never going to forget," Baerga said.

Even Alomar cannot argue with that.

49 Veeck's Trek

When Rick Bay was the club's president in 1992, the Indians held a weekly radio show. Fans could write in questions and Bay would answer them on air. This was a relatively new concept, an untapped form of transparency. It was a tribute to former owner Bill Veeck.

Veeck was not a conventional owner. No one was more open, quirky, eccentric, or over-the-top. He introduced outrageous promotions and unearthed never-before-considered techniques to engage fans. He purchased the Indians in 1946 and immediately boosted the franchise's attendance figures. He moved all of the team's home games to Cleveland Stadium, which could seat 50,000 more fans than League Park could.

"He came out of the war and brought a fun and joy and a little bit of a carnival atmosphere to the world of baseball," said Bob DiBiasio, Indians senior vice president of public affairs. "A remarkable guy."

Veeck served in the Marines for three years during World War II. He suffered an injury that cost him his right leg. He had it amputated and used a wooden leg. As owner of the Indians, he would sit in his office and smoke. He burrowed a little ashtray in the wooden leg and he would bury his cigarette in the small hole that he carved. While he did this, he would leave the door open to his office.

"Any fan, anybody, could walk into Gate A at Cleveland Stadium and walk in and talk to him about the team," DiBiasio said.

Veeck was always trying to be a trendsetter with his gimmicks, his personnel decisions, and his modus operandi. In 1947, he signed Larry Doby, who broke the color barrier in the American League. The following year, he signed Negro Leagues star pitcher Satchel Paige, who contributed to the team's run to a World Series triumph. In 1949, he presided over a funeral at the ballpark to symbolize the end to Cleveland's chances of repeating as champion. After that season, he sold the team to help finance his divorce.

Veeck was inducted into the Baseball Hall of Fame in 1991. He was elected to the Indians' Distinguished Hall of Fame in 2009.

Said DiBiasio: "He was always bringing the fun and excitement."

History of Cleveland Indians Ownership

Charles W. Somers: 1900–1916
Jim Dunn: 1916–1922
Estate of Jim Dunn: 1922–1927
Alva Bradley: 1927–1946
Bill Veeck: 1946–1949
Ellis Ryan: 1949–1952
Myron H. Wilson: 1953–1956
William R. Daley: 1956–1962
Gabe Paul: 1963–1966
Vernon Stouffer: 1967–1972
Nick Mileti: 1972–1976
Ted Bonda: 1977–1978
Steve O'Neill: 1978–1983
Estate of Steve O'Neill: 1983–1986
Dick Jacobs: 1986–2000
Larry Dolan: 2000-present

50 Decisions, Decisions

There was the veteran—the 30-year-old, the two-time All-Star, the guy who had seen the growth of the franchise from a doormat to a championship contender. And then there was the kid—the hot-shot rookie, the 21-year-old who had been in the big leagues for all of four months.

Mike Hargrove had a decision to make. Outwardly, he acted as if there were no decision. Veteran Charles Nagy would be his starter if the Indians and Marlins reached a Game 7 in the 1997 World Series. Inside his mind, however, a storm was brewing. The wheels were spinning. A manager in a postseason series has no choice but to plan ahead and prepare for all contingencies.

Nagy started Game 3 and allowed five runs in six innings. He exited with the Tribe on top 7–5, but the Marlins roared back for a 14–11 win. Jaret Wright held Florida to three runs in six innings in Game 4, which Cleveland claimed 10–3. After that contest, reporters started pressing Hargrove for his Game 7 plan. Orel Hershiser and Chad Ogea would start Games 5 and 6, respectively, either way. Would the reserved veteran Nagy get the call for Game 7, or would it be Wright, the chubby-cheeked kid on three days' rest?

Before Game 5, Hargrove insisted Nagy was his choice.

"As of right now it's Charles Nagy," Hargrove said. "I think we may have a decision to make, but as of right now it's Charles Nagy."

After Game 5, Hargrove's tune changed slightly.

"Officially, right now, it's Charles Nagy in Game 7, if we go that far," Hargrove said. "There are a lot of things that we're going to look at going into that, and the fact of how Jaret can bounce back enters into it. But Game 7, everybody is available for that. So that's why I'm saying that."

Hargrove backed Nagy again before Game 6.

"If we get to Game 7, as of right now we have Charlie penciled in for the start," Hargrove said. "Again, it depends on what happens tonight and who we have to use tonight, whether that happens, but Charlie is, as of right now, the starter for tomorrow."

As he continued to talk, however, he again hedged his bets.

"It depends on if we have to use Charlie Nagy tonight. We may have to use Charlie Nagy, may have to use Wright, [Brian] Anderson, may have to use [Jeff] Juden. It depends on who we use tonight as to who is going to start tomorrow night. As of right now, it's Charles Nagy. I say that leaving my options open. It may not be Nagy, also, but as of right now it is."

The Indians breezed to a 4–1 victory to force Game 7. After Game 6, the second question directed at Hargrove asked for his final decision. The skipper cut to the chase.

"We will start Jaret Wright tomorrow night.

"The performance we got out of him in Game 4 led me to believe that he still is effective and so we will go with Jaret on three days. Last time he had thrown on three days was against the Yankees in the divisional series, and he threw the ball well. We've got everybody available as will the Marlins, too."

Hargrove said he arrived at his decision the day before Game 6, and the way that game unfolded—Ogea and three relievers seamlessly pieced together nine strong innings—solidified his choice. Hargrove had mentioned the idea to Wright a few days earlier and the rookie had little reaction.

"He doesn't let you see him get very excited," Hargrove said. "He has a tremendous will to win. I don't want to get all philosophic, but he handles things real well."

Nagy was disappointed. It was his regular day to pitch. He had been a constant on the team for the entire decade. And now he lost the opportunity of a lifetime to a pitcher with 20 career starts on a big league mound.

"Charlie was so awesome," said Bob DiBiasio, Indians senior vice president of public affairs. "The way he handled Jaret Wright climbing to fame and being the guy to start Game 7, I know it broke his heart, but he handled it as a pro. It's another thing I respect the hell out of that guy for."

Wright, on the other hand, was living out a dream.

"When you dream, you don't dream to pitch in the playoffs, like the first round," he said. "It's always Game 7 of the Series."

Wright authored the best start of his young career. He held the Marlins scoreless on one hit through six innings. In the seventh, Bobby Bonilla took him deep for a leadoff home run. Wright rebounded to punch out Charles Johnson before he walked Craig Counsell and he departed with the Tribe out in front 2–1.

"Being young was a huge advantage for me in that situation," Wright said. "You feel like you're on top of the world."

He would not factor into the decision, of course. The Marlins sent the game into extra innings and tagged Nagy for the winning run in the 11th after a Tony Fernandez error.

"It doesn't eat at me," Wright said. "Life goes on. I was so fortunate to do what I did. It's just a chapter of my life."

51 Once in a Lifetime

Duane Kuiper said if players used walk-up music during his playing days, he would have chosen Three Dog Night's "One Is the Loneliest Number."

There stood Kuiper, in the batter's box, completing his daily practice rituals before a game against the Angels when surly slugger Reggie Jackson yelled loud enough for everyone to hear.

"If I only had one home run, I'd fuckin' quit," Jackson shouted.

Said Kuiper: "That's kind of what I had to live with."

Jackson finished his Hall of Fame career with 563 home runs. Kuiper deposited exactly one ball over the fence in his 3,754 trips to the plate.

So it goes for those with the lanky, lonely digit in the home run column on the back of their baseball cards. Kuiper, who played second base for the Indians from 1974–1981, said he wished he would have socked more than one long ball, but he receives more recognition for his lone round-tripper than he would if he had a less distinguished total in the home run column on the back of his baseball card.

"What's the perfect number after one?" Kuiper said. "Twenty? Would I have rather hit 10 or 20 instead of one? At a certain stage in your life, after it's all said and done, you get mentioned more for hitting one than you did for hitting five."

Plus, the rarity of the event provides Kuiper, now a broadcaster for the San Francisco Giants, with the ability to remember every detail about the night of August 29, 1977. The Indians hosted the Chicago White Sox at Cleveland Stadium in a national telecast that included Al Michaels on play-by-play duties. Michaels is known for his line uttered during the 1980 Olympics: "Do you believe in miracles?" Kuiper, though, said he jokes with Michaels that the line initially earned its acclaim from Kuiper's improbable power stroke.

Cleveland native Steve Stone took the hill for Chicago, with his parents occupying their season seats along the third-base line near the home dugout and on-deck circle. With one out in the bottom of the first, Kuiper turned on a pitch and lifted it to right field. He remembers running to first and seeing the No. 15 on the back of right fielder Wayne Nordhagen's uniform. He wasn't accustomed to that sight, since he rarely hit the ball over an outfielder's head.

"I thought, 'You know what? This maybe has a chance to get out of the park,'" Kuiper said.

The baseball landed on the other side of the right-field fence. Kuiper had never engaged in a home run trot before, so he sprinted around the bases.

"If I could do something different," Kuiper said, "I would have definitely slowed it down a little bit."

Buddy Bell, the next batter and one of Kuiper's favorite teammates, greeted him at home plate.

Kuiper never clubbed another pitch over the outfield wall, but he tagged Stone again three years later. On September 9, 1981, at Memorial Stadium in Baltimore, Kuiper belted a pitch off the right-field fence. The ball bounced back into the field of play and Kuiper ended up on second base with an RBI double.

"At the time, I was really disappointed," Kuiper said. "I would've loved to have a home run. I think had it bounced over the fence, Stone probably would have committed suicide."

After the ensuing hitter, Mike Fischlin, singled to left to give the Indians a 3–0 lead, Dave Ford replaced Stone on the mound. As Stone retreated to the Orioles' dugout, he passed Kuiper, who had advanced to third base on Fischlin's base knock. Kuiper intentionally avoided making eye contact with Stone. Instead, he turned his back to the sauntering pitcher and peered toward the outfield.

"I liked him," Kuiper said. "He was a good guy. I didn't want him to have to say anything to me and I didn't want to have to say anything to him."

When he was not facing Stone, Kuiper did not have much of a power stroke at the plate. Tribe manager Frank Robinson stressed that Kuiper not attempt to hit the ball in the air on any occasion. Kuiper contends that the skipper's mandate only reinforced what the infielder already knew: power was not his game.

"Guys around the league respected me, whether I hit one or whether I hit 30," Kuiper said. "I always said I was a regular player for all those years and only hit one home run, so I was doing something right."

52 Pick Your Favorite Condiment in the Hot Dog Derby

The Brewers have their sausage race. The Nationals have their presidential race. The Indians host the Hot Dog Derby.

After the completion of the fifth inning of every home game, three condiments enter the field from a gate in the left-field wall and sprint—or, sometimes, skip, hop, or dance—around the diamond until they reach the finish line in foul territory near first base. It is a heated, spirited competition, one that involves the team mascot, Slider; an actual rulebook to which each participant must adhere; foreign objects; and plenty of creativity.

Here is a rundown of the daily contestants:

Ketchup: The mischievous alpha-male of the group. Ketchup, with his crooked glasses and devious smile, is notorious for trying to win at all costs. He can often be seen cheating by cutting across the infield grass to shorten his route to the finish line. Therefore, Ketchup is typically Slider's target when the mascot interferes and flexes his muscles to create a level playing field.

Mustard: The steady, honest racer. Mustard, who sports a sideways ball cap topped with a pinwheel, isn't high on gimmicks or ruthless abandon. While Ketchup devises methods to attain an upper hand, Mustard prefers to put his head down and focus on the finish line. As a result, he is often the beneficiary when Slider eliminates Ketchup with a tackle or a swing of the bat to the bun.

Onion: She's the eye candy of the bunch and she has been known to use it to her advantage. On more than one occasion, she has darted across the finish line while Ketchup or Mustard is caught ogling her. She carries a purse at all times, though the handbag often doubles as a weapon at the most convenient moments.

The winner of the race is predetermined, though the humans in the costumes are given creative license to set up a compelling contest. In 2011, the three hot dogs each claimed 27 victories to end the season in a three-way tie. The 2014 competition came down to the final race of the season, which Mustard won. The scoreboard at Progressive Field asks fans to vote for who they think will cross the finish line first. The estimates are revealed before the contestants emerge from the base of the left-field wall.

Some members of the Indians have been known take it a bit further. During the 2009 season, closer Kerry Wood and bullpen catcher Dave Wallace bet on the competition on a daily basis. Wood, however, had an advantage: He would get a heating pack and begin his stretching routine in the stadium tunnels in the fifth inning. On his walk to the bullpen, he would pass the three hot dogs, who would be waiting to enter the field. Wood often

Onion, Mustard, and Ketchup try to beat one another in the always heated Hot Dog Derby. The race takes place after the fifth inning at every Indians home game.

conversed with them to get information on who was bound to win that day's race.

Similar races have sprouted up around the league. The trend started with the Brewers' sausage race. A bratwurst, Polish sausage, Italian sausage, hot dog, and chorizo duke it out at Miller Park each game. On July 9, 2003, Pirates first baseman Randall Simon struck the Italian sausage with a bat, causing the competitor to fall to the ground. Simon earned a fine and a three-game suspension from the league and a fine for disorderly conduct.

53 Grover

Mike Hargrove, or Grover, had the task of making sure a clubhouse full of ticking time bombs didn't explode. He had to oversee a group of confident players who carried themselves with a palpable swagger, guys who admitted that they knew they were going to win when they stepped onto the field.

The winning part wasn't the most demanding facet of the manager's job. Not during the regular season, at least. The Indians captured five consecutive American League Central Division crowns from 1995–1999 with Hargrove at the helm. The talent on the roster alone translated into victories. But Hargrove had to guarantee that that talent didn't interfere with daily business. He had to ensure that a clubhouse oozing with ego didn't collapse.

"He doesn't get anywhere near the accolades he deserves for keeping that collection of personalities together," said Bob DiBiasio, Indians senior vice president of public affairs.

Hargrove spent the second half of his playing career with the Indians, from 1979–1985. He hit .292 with Cleveland and logged a .396 on-base percentage. He batted .300 or better in each of his first three seasons with the Tribe. He also developed a reputation as a hitter who capitalized on the game's timelessness. Hargrove often stalled by stepping out of the batter's box to readjust his batting gloves, helmet, or any other gadget that could possibly require realignment. That attribute earned him the nickname "The Human Rain Delay."

Perhaps all of that fine-tuning foreshadowed a successful managerial career. Hargrove oversaw a roster of young players who blossomed into All-Stars. He took over at the helm for John McNamara in 1991. In the spring of 1993, Hargrove steered the organization through the boating tragedy that claimed the lives of relief pitchers Steve Olin and Tim Crews.

"We had a team full, a locker room full of very, very young players that had not been through anything like that," said former general manager John Hart. "This was a club that had been together for two or three years. There was not a free agent on that ball club in '93. These were all kids. And I think it allowed Grover to perhaps do some of the things he does best, which is allow his character, his caring, to show."

After a pair of 76–86 seasons, the Tribe made the leap in 1994. Unfortunately, the player's strike cut the season short. In 1995, however, as the Indians established themselves as baseball's most loaded and dangerous team—and the players in the clubhouse knew it—Hargrove pushed the right buttons. Cleveland finished with a league-best 100–44 record and pushed the Atlanta Braves to six games in the World Series, the franchise's first appearance in the Fall Classic in four decades.

"[Hargrove] not winning the Manager of the Year award in '95 was a travesty," DiBiasio said. "Our guys won 100 out of 144. And he doesn't win Manager of the Year? It makes no sense. Just because we're a talented team? It wasn't something where you and I could have managed that team to 100 wins."

The Indians qualified for the postseason in each of the final five years of Hargrove's tenure in Cleveland. He was dismissed after the 1999 American League Division Series, in which the Indians blew a 2–0 series lead and bowed out, again falling short of a league title, despite five straight division championships.

During Hargrove's time as Tribe skipper, he captained a roster full of hotheads, divas, and personalities. His relaxed temperament helped mesh a group of All-Stars who carried All-Star egos. He challenged the collection of star power to etch its name into franchise lore. When people look back at the most prolific stretch of Indians baseball, they note that Hargrove served as the lead man for those teams.

"He was a big part of it," said team president Mark Shapiro. "I'm not sure any one person gets credit, but Mike was a guy who understood the personality and nature of the team and understood how to keep a calm, steady hand on the rudder and kept the team going in the right direction and did what he had to do. Some of that is making sure the talent actually produces and plays. Maybe that gets overlooked, but there is talent in that, too."

54 Bye Bye, Cy

Victor Martinez sat at his locker, tears streaming down his face.

Earlier that day, 4-year-old Victor Jose had asked his father: "Daddy, are we still an Indian?"

Martinez told his son: "So far." But so far only lasted so long.

After coming within one victory of a trip to the World Series in 2007, the Indians fell so hard, so fast, that two years later, the club had started from scratch. The tears shed by the father and son in the Indians' clubhouse resembled what many inside—and outside—the Indians' organization felt about trading away one of the franchise's centerpieces and about how close the team had come to a championship but how far it now stood from one, less than two years later.

It started with CC Sabathia. The burly left-hander was slated to become a free agent after the 2008 campaign. He sought loads of cash the Indians could not afford. He was destined for a big market and was operating on borrowed time in Cleveland. So, when the Indians dragged out of the gate in '08, dealing Sabathia seemed to be their most sensible strategy.

The Indians drafted Sabathia in the first round of the 1998 amateur draft out of high school. He debuted with the Tribe at the start of the 2001 campaign, when he was a 20-year-old rookie. That season, he amassed a 17–5 record and 4.39 ERA, with 171 strikeouts in 180⅓ innings, as he finished second in the balloting for American League Rookie of the Year. He eventually blossomed into the anchor of the club's starting rotation, as evidenced by his three All-Star Game selections and his 2007 American League Cy Young Award, earned after a 19–7 showing, 3.21 ERA, and league-high 241 innings.

Once the team sputtered at the start of the '08 season, the writing on the wall became clear. The Indians were going to lose Sabathia in a matter of months, anyway. They needed to get something in return while they could. After weeks of speculation, the club shipped him to Milwaukee for powerful first base prospect Matt LaPorta, pitchers Zach Jackson and Rob Bryson, and a player to be named later, which became eventual All-Star left fielder Michael Brantley. Jackson and Bryson never amounted to much at the major league level. LaPorta, the crown jewel of the deal from Cleveland's perspective, fizzled in the big leagues. Brantley's inclusion salvaged the trade for the Tribe.

The exchange signaled the end of the brief window of contention the Indians had initiated the previous season. They sunk lower a year later.

"Those things are difficult because they defy your competitive nature," said team president Mark Shapiro, then the organization's general manager. "You operationally understand the challenges and you start to say, 'I guess this is the model that we're going to have to always be in, that churn cycle where we play the window out and if we feel like the window might be closing, we need to be opportunistic to get assets back in and players back in so we're not losing for eight to 10 years.' We really wanted to stay out of those long-term valleys and try to turn things around as quickly as possible."

Shapiro continued wheeling and dealing in 2009. Cliff Lee spent his first eight big league seasons with the Indians following his relocation from Montreal in the Bartolo Colon trade in 2002. In 2008, the southpaw compiled a sparkling stat line, with a 22–3 record, a 2.54 ERA, and a pair of complete-game shutouts. All of the production merited him the distinction of starting the All-Star Game for the American League squad and earning the league's Cy Young Award. As the Indians struggled through the 2009 season, however, his name came up in trade rumors. He was scheduled to hit the free-agent market after the 2010 campaign. The Indians did not have the funds, nor the win-now mentality, to lock Lee up long-term. Two days before the July 31 non-waiver trade deadline, the Tribe dealt Lee and outfielder Ben Francisco to the Phillies for minor league pitchers Jason Knapp and Carlos Carrasco, infielder Jason Donald, and catcher Lou Marson.

The Indians considered Knapp the prized acquisition in the exchange. There was one problem: The righty's pitching shoulder was in shambles. Knapp was on the disabled list at the time of the trade. He ended up needing two operations and never advanced past Class A ball before the Indians released him in August 2012.

Knapp went nearly four years without pitching professionally before he returned for the Texas Rangers' Class A affiliate in 2014.

Lee and Sabathia opposed each other on the mound in Game 1 of the 2009 World Series, when Sabathia's New York Yankees squared off against Lee's Phillies.

Two days after the Lee trade, the Indians' front office struck again. Martinez—whom the organization had signed as a 17-year-old shortstop out of Venezuela in 1996—had spent parts of eight seasons in the middle of the team's batting order and earned three trips to the Midsummer Classic. He was moved to Boston for pitchers Justin Masterson, Nick Hagadone, and Bryan Price. Martinez was not shy about his adoration for the Indians' organization. He became the heart and soul of the clubhouse and the lineup. Now he had to leave the only franchise he had ever known. Martinez called it the toughest day of his career.

"We were trading a lot of those guys who were great guys, guys like Victor who meant so much to us personally, guys we had believed in so completely and totally," Shapiro said. "That's hard. You never get past the personal nature of trading a player that you care about and believe in."

55 Web Gem

Ask Omar Vizquel for his choice on the greatest play he ever made in the field and he will hem and haw for a moment before opting for the one with the best timing. His manager, Mike Hargrove, was getting a drink of water when the ball was hit to the shortstop.

"I saw Omar dive and make the play and I almost choked," Hargrove said.

It came in Game 6 of the 1997 World Series. On a hazy night in South Florida, the Indians grasped a 4–1 lead in the sixth inning. The Marlins had runners on second and third with two outs and Mike Jackson was pitching with Charles Johnson at the plate. Johnson pulled Jackson's offering into the hole between short and third. Vizquel laid out, his chest smacking the grass beyond the infield dirt. He stretched out his left arm to corral the sharply hit grounder. At that time, Gary Sheffield was waltzing toward the plate. Jim Eisenreich was more than halfway to third. Had the ball skirted past Vizquel, two runs would have scored.

Instead, the limber shortstop propped himself up with his left knee and fired the baseball across his body toward first base. When he let go, his back foot was in the outfield grass. His front foot was gracing the edge of the infield dirt. His throw struck Jim Thome's glove on a line drive to retire Johnson and end the inning. The Indians maintained their 4–1 advantage.

"Nothing that Omar does with his glove surprises me," Hargrove said after the game. "Nothing he does with his bare hands surprises me. This guy has got the guts of a burglar. And he's very, very good at what he does and is very cool and collected. He's a player."

Vizquel took off his hat as he jogged off the field. His teammates and coaches left their spots on the bench to greet him upon his return to the dugout.

On the national telecast, Hall of Fame second baseman Joe Morgan, who won five Gold Glove Awards himself, said: "You don't win Gold Gloves if you can't make the great plays under pressure."

56 Quite Frankly

The temperature hovered around freezing on Opening Day in 1975, when the Indians hosted the New York Yankees at Cleveland Stadium. Nearly 57,000 fans braved the conditions and sat in thier seats around the tundra to watch Frank Robinson, the league's first African American manager, direct the Indians in his first game. Robinson, a two-time Most Valuable Player award winner—once in each league, the first player to accomplish that feat—came over in a trade with the California Angels near the end of the 1974 campaign.

He became manager prior to the 1975 season and, despite settling into a reserve role, was still a player at the time. He inserted himself into the No. 2 spot in the Opening Day lineup on April 8. In his first at-bat, he launched a solo home run to left field off of right-hander Doc Medich. The Indians proceeded to claim a 5–3 victory.

Not only did Robinson have to deal with daily managerial rigors and extra attention for his trailblazing achievement, but he had to balance his own playing time and keep his players' egos in check.

In his Baseball Hall of Fame induction speech in 1982, Robinson quipped: "If I had wanted to go after personal goals I could have inserted myself into the lineup much more often in Cleveland when I was a player-manager, but as a manager I had better sense than that. I knew I had better ballplayers than Frank Robinson at that time so I played the best that I had."

Of course, he adhered to his hunches from time to time. On June 11, 1976, Robinson called upon himself to pinch-hit in the bottom of the 13th inning. The Chicago White Sox had taken a

4–3 lead in the top half of the frame. With two outs and a runner on third, Robinson batted for Orlando Gonzalez and clubbed a walk-off home run. It was one of only three home runs he hit that season, his last as a player. He finished his career with 586 home runs, fourth-most in history at the time of his retirement.

Robinson managed the Indians from 1975–1977 and finished with a 186–189 record. He would eventually manage the San Francisco Giants, Baltimore Orioles, and Montreal Expos/Washington Nationals. During his presidency, Gerald Ford once sent Robinson a telegram commending him on becoming the first African American manager in baseball history.

57 Rally Alley

The Indians were dejected. The flight back to Cleveland from Atlanta was long—much longer, it seemed, than the hour and a half it actually took. After a 100-win regular season, the Indians came up short against the Braves in six games in the 1995 World Series. They mustered only one hit off Tom Glavine and Co. in the series-deciding contest, a 1–0 loss. To come so close, after a 41-year World Series (and postseason) drought, was agonizing. The accomplishments accumulated throughout a magical season were placed on the back burner.

Then, the plane landed.

The team received a police escort from the airport back to Jacobs Field. Cars pulled over on I-71. People exited those cars and applauded the team busses as they whizzed past. Hordes of fans greeted the team downtown and at the ballpark. They were not dwelling in the demoralization of a Fall Classic defeat. They were proud of the leaps forward taken by a franchise that had been mired in dreadfulness for four decades.

"We were disheartened," said Jim Thome, then the club's third baseman. "We wanted to win a World Series. I think what put it in perspective is how our fans showed up."

Two days after Game 6, the city of Cleveland hosted a rally to celebrate the Indians' season. Thousands of fans poured out into Public Square, the center of downtown, where a giant stage was set up for Tribe players, coaches, and executives. Player banners adorned every light post in front of the Terminal Tower. Fans brought signs and donned Indians garb for the chilly, overcast Monday afternoon celebration.

A group of police on motorcycles first carved a path down Superior Road, adjacent to Public Square. A row of police on horseback followed. Next came a line of cars, followed by a series of high school marching bands and cheerleaders. Band members had players' names and numbers inscribed on their instruments. One tuba bore the name Belle and the numeral eight. A few appropriately adorned trucks drove past. One displayed a banner that read "Wahoo, what a season! Wahoo, what a finish!! Wahoo, what a TEAM!!!" There was persistent screaming and chanting and ringing of cowbells.

As the players took the stage, fans jockeyed for position to get the best possible view. One person even climbed a cylinder post to stand atop the crosswalk sign. Others stood atop newspaper stands, all to catch a glimpse of their heroes of the diamond. It was the start of what blossomed into the golden era of Indians baseball. It was a telltale sign of an attachment between the fan base and team. On this day, no one could tell that the Indians had actually lost the World Series. Everyone was just appreciative of what had been achieved. The team generated that kind of response just by reaching the Fall Classic. Now, they had a taste of what the ensuing years would bring.

"It was overwhelmingly positive, the feeling," Thome said. "I think at that point, we as players knew, 'Wow. Our fans are really behind us and we have something special here.'"

58 Hard-Headed

Twenty-one years after it happened, Jose Canseco posted a message on his personal Twitter account.

"Poor ball was never the same," he wrote.

Canseco laughed at it at the time and he poked fun at himself years after the matter. With video evidence available for all to see, what else is he to do?

On May 26, 1993, in the Indians' final season at Cleveland Stadium, Tribe designated hitter Carlos Martinez skied a fly ball to right field in the bottom of the fourth inning. As Canseco rushed back toward the wall in right field, he looked up to locate the baseball and it promptly bounced off the top of his head and over the fence. Martinez was awarded a home run, a solo shot that narrowed the Texas Rangers' lead to 3–2. The Indians eventually emerged with a 7–6 victory.

The following day, *The Plain Dealer* ran the headline: "CONK! The Tribe Wins By A Head." As the ball struck Canseco's dome, the right fielder stumbled into the blue-padded wall and fell to the ground. Once he returned to his feet, he surveyed the area and tried to figure out how such a comical series of events had unfolded. He laughed it all off. Canseco said after the game that he did not know what had happened.

At one point in 2013, Major League Baseball's website, MLB.com, posted a slow-motion video of the play when its pages

1993: A ball hit by Carlos Martinez bounces off the head of outfielder Jose Canseco and over the wall at Cleveland Stadium, which resulted in an Indians home run.

malfunctioned, to symbolize an error with the site. The play has lived on as the top selection on just about every baseball blooper reel.

From the moment the baseball caromed off of his cranium, Canseco knew the play would live in infamy. He quipped that he would be on the highlight shows for the ensuing month and said: "I guess I'm just an entertainer."

The Indians proceeded to score twice more in the fourth inning on a two-out, two-run single by Felix Fermin. They increased their 4–3 lead with three more runs in the sixth and they hung on, as the Rangers tacked on a run in each of the final three innings. Cleveland won by one run. Was Canseco's blunder the difference? His hard-headedness certainly did not help.

59 Honoring a Legend

Anne Feller stood atop the mound before a sold-out Progressive Field crowd on a chilly April afternoon. She then knelt down in front of the white No. 19 scripted in the dirt behind the rubber, where she placed a baseball before walking off the field.

One day after her husband, Hall of Fame hurler Bob Feller, was memorialized at a service in Cleveland, Anne capped a pregame ceremony honoring the Indians' all-time wins leader. During the team's pregame routine, each player sported a No. 19 uniform adorned with a patch displaying the hurler in his patented high-leg-kick windup motion. The patches remained on the club's jerseys throughout the 2011 campaign.

About an hour before first pitch, the Indians hung a pair of banners and a giant Feller uniform over the left-field wall. One

Surprising Ending

The Indians hosted the Detroit Tigers at the end of the 1940 season. Cleveland needed to sweep the three-game series to clinch the American League pennant. The Tigers needed one win to eliminate the Tribe and capture the pennant themselves.

Cleveland turned to Bob Feller for the first game. The right-hander had amassed 27 victories, including an Opening Day no-hitter. The Tigers countered with relatively unknown hurler Floyd Giebell, who had made 10 career appearances, nine out of the bullpen. Tigers manager Del Baker wanted to save his aces—Bobo Newsom and Schoolboy Rowe—for the two games in which Feller was not taking the hill.

Giebell twirled a six-hit shutout. Feller allowed only three hits in nine innings, but he served up a two-run home run to Rudy York for the only scoring in the contest. The Tigers' 2–0 triumph propelled Detroit to the World Series. The final two games of the three-game set at Cleveland Stadium meant nothing. The Indians won both.

Feller won another 184 games during his prestigious Hall of Fame career. Giebell never won another major league game.

of the banners showed a portrait of a young, smiling Feller in his military uniform. The day after the Japanese bombed Pearl Harbor in 1941, Feller put his baseball career on hold and enlisted in the Navy. He served for four years. The other banner showed Feller in that windup, his body arched back, his right arm reaching toward the dirt on the mound, his left leg lifted high in the air, ready to deliver one of his 100-mph fastballs, a blazing pitch known as the "Heater from Van Meter," named after his hometown in Iowa.

"Bob gave his life and soul to the Cleveland Indians," said manager Manny Acta. "No one will ever be associated with the Cleveland Indians the way Bob has been."

On March 31, 2011, at a memorial service for Feller—attended by four Tribe players, a host of Indians brass, and hundreds of others—team owner Paul Dolan, Governor of Ohio John Kasich, and Jeff Idelson, president of the Baseball Hall of Fame, shared anecdotes about the man who racked up 266 wins in an Indians uniform. Feller died on December 15, 2010, at the age of 92. The day after the memorial service, after Anne Feller deposited the baseball in the dirt, Fausto Carmona scooped it up, and another Opening Day was under way. The timing was fitting, given that Feller stakes claim to the most heralded Opening Day feat in baseball history.

On April 16, 1940, a 21-year-old Feller tossed the only Opening Day no-hitter in major league lore, as he blanked the Chicago White Sox in a 1–0 win at Comiskey Park. Feller walked five. Another reached base when center fielder Roy Weatherly misplayed a fly ball in the second inning. Other than that, the right-hander proved unflappable.

60 Justice for All

The Indians could not manage a hit, let alone a run. So how were they going to overcome David Justice's solo home run in the sixth inning of Game 6 of the 1995 World Series? Southpaw Tom Glavine worked the corners of the plate—maybe even the corners of the corners—and kept the Tribe hitters off-balance with a bevy of change-ups. His dominance fueled the Atlanta Braves to a World Series title and forced the Indians to keep searching for their first championship since 1948.

Aside from a pair of walks issued to imposing slugger Albert Belle, Glavine kept the Tribe off the base paths until Tony Pena guided a softly struck single to center to lead off the top of the sixth. Cleveland left-hander Jim Poole, who relieved starter Dennis Martinez in the previous frame and struck out Fred McGriff on three pitches, stepped to the plate with instructions to execute a sacrifice bunt and advance Pena into scoring position. Poole had never registered a major league at-bat. Just about every pitcher practices bunting at some point during the season. Still, manager Mike Hargrove could have turned to one of his bench players to carry out the task or a pitcher with National League experience, such as Orel Hershiser.

Hargrove, however, wanted Poole to pitch to lefties David Justice and Ryan Klesko in the bottom half of the inning, despite having southpaws Alan Embree and Paul Assenmacher also at his disposal. So, Poole trotted out to the plate, bunted three consecutive pitches foul and retreated to the dugout. The Indians failed to score. They never got another chance.

Poole returned to the mound in the bottom of the sixth to complete his assignment. Justice, who had created a rift between himself and the Braves' fan base after criticizing their support of the team a day earlier, led off the inning. Poole started him with a fastball away for a strike. His second pitch, another heater, sailed out of the zone. Poole tried to come inside with another fastball, but Justice turned on it and deposited it over the right-field fence. Justice raised his right arm as he sprinted out of the batter's box. Once he rounded first base and the ball landed past the blue wall, he pumped his left fist. The fans quickly forgave him. Justice was served. The crowd's bellowing of the Tomahawk Chop echoed throughout the stadium. The Braves had their run. Glavine had all the backing he needed.

Atlanta closer Mark Wohlers put the finishing touches on the shutout. Pena's harmless single proved to be Cleveland's only base knock. As soon as Marquis Grissom squeezed Carlos Baerga's fly ball for the final out, the Braves commenced their celebration on the diamond. Many of the Indians remained in the dugout and watched. Some wept. Some stared out into oblivion, wondering where it all went wrong, how the league's most prolific offense had gone quiet at the most critical juncture and how long the Indians would have to wait for their own championship celebration.

61 Super Joe

They told stories that built up his legendary status, tales about him opening beer bottles with his eye socket, yanking his own tooth with pliers, removing an unwelcome tattoo with a razor blade, and consuming alcoholic beverages through his nose. They marveled at his hitting prowess. This kid, who turned 25 mid-season, stood toe-to-toe with the American League's pitching elite and racked up numbers that earned him the Rookie of the Year award.

The ride on which Joe Charboneau took Cleveland in 1980 ended rather abruptly. The rush and the jolt he provided the team and the city swiftly fizzled. Charboneau never duplicated that unforgettable rookie campaign. In fact, after just a few short years, he never even had the chance to come close.

Charboneau burned bridges with the Philadelphia Phillies, who had selected the outfielder in the second round in 1976. The Indians took a chance on him and he batted .352 for Double-A Chattanooga in 1979. The following spring, a litany of injuries paved the way for him to make the Opening Day roster, even though a fan in Mexico stabbed him in the side with a pen knife while he signed autographs before an exhibition in early March.

Charboneau quickly won over the media and the fans in Cleveland. His bat did much of the talking—he hovered near the .300 mark for most of the season before finishing with a .289 average, 23 home runs, and 87 RBIs. His crazy, unfathomable stories did the rest. At one point, the legend of the phenom grew so large that a song, titled "Go Joe Charboneau" reached No. 3 on the local music charts.

Who's the newest guy in town?
Go Joe Charboneau
Turns the ballpark upside down
Go Joe Charboneau
Who do we appreciate?
Go Joe Charboneau
Fits right in with the other eight?
Go Joe Charboneau
Who's the one to keep our hopes alive?
Go Joe Charboneau
Straight from the seventh to the pennant drive?
Go Joe Charboneau
Raise your glass, let out a cheer
Go Joe Charboneau
For Cleveland's Rookie of the Year
Go Joe Charboneau

Charboneau soaked up the attention. He did not care for the "Super Joe" nickname or the hyperbolizing of some of the tales of his eccentric ways, but the support was overwhelming. The positive recognition was short-lived, however.

After Charboneau garnered the Rookie of the Year award for his performance in 1980, he injured his back sliding into second base the ensuing spring training. He played through pain, but after he batted just .210 with four home runs through 48 games, the Indians demoted him to Triple-A Charleston. There, he hit just .217 in 14 contests. He underwent a procedure on his back after the season. In 1982, he needed another operation after re-injuring his back.

Had he suffered from the dreaded Sophomore Jinx? Was he merely a flash in the pan to begin with? Had his off-the-field antics caught up to him? Was he simply the victim of a handful of career-debilitating injuries?

Charboneau's last major league at-bat came on June 1, 1982, less than two years after he took home hardware as the American League's top rookie. The Pittsburgh Pirates gave him an opportunity in 1984, but he hit just .224 in 15 games at Triple-A Hawaii. While there, he appeared in the movie *The Natural* as an extra (he played one of Roy Hobbs' teammates on the New York Knights).

Charboneau has tried as hard as possible to keep baseball in his life. He coached in independent leagues, gave lessons, and ran clinics. He served as an alumni ambassador for the Indians. He also has maintained his presence in Cleveland as a hitting coach for the Lorain County Ironmen, a summer collegiate team in the Prospect League. In February 2014, the Lake Erie Crushers of the Frontier League hired him as a hitting instructor.

62 A Banner Season

The 2007 season was a banner year for the Indians. It did not end with a World Series banner, but the team came awfully close and the widespread organizational success signified the culmination of what the club had been working toward since it initiated a rebuilding process five years earlier.

Center fielder Grady Sizemore won a Gold Glove award. Burly southpaw CC Sabathia took home the American League Cy Young Award. Eric Wedge was named American League Manager of the Year. General manager Mark Shapiro was recognized as Executive of the Year.

The Indians had improved their win total in 2004 and again in 2005. They tumbled, however, in 2006, when they finished fourth in the American League Central and dropped from 93 wins to 78.

The 2007 season was the perfect storm. At first, it was a literal snowstorm, one that wiped out the team's first home series. But by the time summer heat swept through Cleveland, the Indians had ascended to the top of the division, the American League and, in the end, all of baseball. Their 96 wins tied them with the Boston Red Sox for most in the league.

They got off to a blazing start, with a 14–8 mark in April, an atypical first month for Wedge's Cleveland teams. For much of the summer, they jockeyed back and forth with the Detroit Tigers for possession of first place in the division. They used an eight-game winning streak at the end of August to attain a 5½-game lead over the Tigers. When the clubs met at Jacobs Field for a three-game set beginning September 17, Detroit all but needed a sweep to have any shot at displacing the Tribe.

In the first game of the series, the Tigers took a 5–2 lead into the eighth inning. Cleveland carved into the deficit when Victor Martinez plated a run with a groundout. Jhonny Peralta then swatted an opposite-field blast to right off of Joel Zumaya to tie the contest. The Indians won the game on a Casey Blake walk-off home run in the 11th. The deflating loss crushed Detroit's hopes. The Indians proceeded to sweep the series and build an insurmountable division lead.

On September 23, Rafael Betancourt struck out Oakland's Mark Ellis for the final out before a Sunday afternoon crowd of 40,250. The outfielders sprinted in toward the pitcher's mound. Players poured out of the dugout and onto the infield. Martinez jumped into Betancourt's arms. Streamers and fireworks filled the sky. The Indians had clinched the division and their first playoff berth in six years.

63 Selby vs. Rivera

Tom Hamilton's voice could have shattered glass.

The Indians' radio play-by-play man erupted as Bill Selby lined one of Mariano Rivera's cutters to right field. The Indians had narrowed a 7–0 deficit to 7–6 on July 14, 2002, and it was up to Selby to provide the knockout punch against the most celebrated closer in Major League Baseball history.

He did. Or so it seemed. An ecstatic Hamilton shouted as Selby socked Rivera's offering, but there was one problem: The supposed walk-off hit landed in foul territory.

"It looked like a game-winner," Hamilton said. "I thought it was a fair ball. You always remember your mistakes."

Hamilton apologized, though who could blame him? There hadn't been much to scream about in excitement during the 2002 campaign. The moment came during the first season of the Indians' rebuilding process, one that abruptly halted the greatest stretch of baseball in franchise history.

After a seven-year period in which the Indians captured six American League Central Division crowns, advanced to a pair of World Series, and filled the ballpark to capacity on a nightly basis, this was a new era. It was uncharted territory and the initial results were tough to swallow.

On this particular Sunday afternoon, the Indians had mounted a respectable comeback against the titans of the American League. A moral victory amid a murky season would have sufficed. Wins and losses wouldn't define the 2002 club, anyway; the reconstruction of the organizational roster would.

So, after Selby's near-walk-off veered foul, reality set in. Selby entered the game with a .219 batting average, zero home runs, and three RBIs in 18 games for the Indians that season. He would eventually finish a five-year big league career with a .223 average and 11 home runs in 198 games.

The 5'9" Mississippi kid with the blonde buzz cut didn't stand a chance against Rivera, who five days earlier had thrown a scoreless inning for the American League in the All-Star Game. Rivera retired after the 2013 season, having earned 13 All-Star team nods, tallied a major league record 652 saves and logged a career ERA of 2.21. Rivera served up four grand slams in his 1,115 big league appearances. He hadn't allowed one in nearly seven years.

"You don't remember them all, but I remember that one," Hamilton said. "First off because it's Mariano Rivera, and it's Bill Selby! Nothing against Bill Selby, but usually in that situation, after you hit what looked to be a game-winner, then you strike out and the game is over. Everyone says 'Oh, Bill, you came so close.'

"And then he actually did it."

Selby pulled a 2–2 cutter to right field. Hamilton erupted again. This one wasn't curving foul. It nestled into the right-field seats to the right of the visitor's bullpen at Jacobs Field. The Indians won 10–7. An innocent, unimposing Selby forever entrenched his name into franchise lore.

It marked the first walk-off home run Rivera had ever surrendered. Rivera never allowed more runs (six) in a relief appearance.

In the middle of a season highlighted by transition, redirection and a harsh dose of reality, the Indians finally had reason to celebrate.

"That was tough," said team president Mark Shapiro, then in his first year as the club's general manager. "That's probably a great memory for Bill and a cool positive for us. When you're heading into waters like that, you have to know that you have to hold onto those great moments. They're important. You have to enjoy them."

Selby's blast boosted the Tribe's record to 41–49, as he handed Joel Skinner his second victory in four games as manager after taking over for Charlie Manuel, who received a mid-season pink slip. The Yankees entered the affair 16½ games better than the Indians. As improbable as it was to foresee a Tribe triumph when Cleveland trailed 7–0, who could have envisioned such a ninth-inning finish?

"I remember at one point looking out at the mound and there was a shorter pitcher and Selby was playing shortstop," Shapiro said. "We had all short guys and I'm like, 'Holy cow. How far have we come from the big dudes that were playing for us?' We were taking pride in just battling.

"That game, that's the beauty of baseball. In any one moment, anything can happen."

64 Great Sock-cess

The Indians' surge to the World Series in 1997 often overshadows their pedestrian showing during the regular season. Mike Hargrove's bunch wobbled to an 86–75 mark, as the Tribe captured the American League Central crown by a six-game margin. The division title was in doubt until early September. The Indians finished with the fewest wins of any division champion in the American League. They finished with 10 fewer wins than the New York Yankees, who earned the American League Wild Card berth.

Cleveland treaded water until late August. The team needed a spark. First baseman Jim Thome was known to hike up his pant legs and display his high socks when he played. So, on Thome's 27th birthday on August 27, shortstop Omar Vizquel spearheaded a clubhouse movement that required everyone to make a collective fashion statement.

A Triumphant Homecoming

The whispers circulated throughout the Indians clubhouse on the afternoon of August 26, 2011. The Tribe had re-acquired Jim Thome a day earlier. Initially, his new teammates tossed about the idea of sporting high socks—in honor of Thome's patented look—on his birthday, August 27.

In 1997, the Indians began wearing high socks on Thome's birthday. They won that day and, subsequently, rode the fashion wave to a World Series appearance.

They couldn't wait until his birthday in 2011, however. According to reliever Joe Smith, certain players whined, "I don't look good in high socks" and "I have 'cankles.'" Still, the players pulled up their red socks as they took the field.

"I thought it looked great," Smith said. "Everybody, coaches included, did it. Maybe it means something, maybe it doesn't, but I thought it was pretty cool. He definitely deserves that for what he's done for the game."

The wardrobe adjustment worked; the Indians won on August 26. They won again the next day, as Thome launched a home run on his 41st birthday.

Thome appreciated the gesture.

"It was very nice," he said. "It was similar to '97."

The players all sported their high socks that night against the Angels at Anaheim Stadium. A 10-run inning—fueled by Matt Williams' three-run home run and three-run double—provided the club with a 10–4 win. Ironically, Thome had the night off. As superstition mandates, the Indians could not ditch the wardrobe choice after such a successful offensive outburst. So, the team maintained its fashion stance in its next game two days later against the Cubs. The Indians won 7–6. The socks stuck around. After a loss, the team rattled off a couple more victories. Another loss was followed by a five-game winning streak. After the implementation of the dress code, the Indians won nine of 11. The stretch enhanced their lead in the American League Central by three more games. By the second week of September, they sat somewhat comfortably atop the division totem pole.

The team marched all the way to the World Series, an enthralling, seven-game bout that the Florida Marlins claimed in dramatic, gut-wrenching fashion. It was fashion itself, though, that spurred the Tribe in the home stretch of the 1997 campaign. Frankly, the Indians seemed relatively average that season. The roster underwent a litany of modifications. The lineup lost its most powerful punch when Albert Belle cashed in on a hefty pay day with the White Sox in November 1996. It added veteran third baseman Matt Williams, which forced Thome to relocate to the other side of the infield. One week before the start of the regular season, the team traded reliever Alan Embree and All-Star center fielder Kenny Lofton to Atlanta for outfielders Marquis Grissom and David Justice. Grissom and Williams struggled for much of the regular season while growing accustomed to the American League.

"We did make some very difficult decisions," said general manager John Hart. "I think some very probably controversial calls, starting with the Carlos Baerga trade, the decision to let Albert Belle go, and then obviously the Kenny Lofton trade. And we knew that we were bringing in some different types of players, very talented players that were changing leagues."

Aside from April, when they posted a 12–13 mark, the Indians finished every month with a winning record. But the best record they amassed in any month was May's 15–11 showing. They certainly were not the well-oiled machine they were a year earlier, when they registered a 99–62 mark. They barely resembled the team that rolled to a 100–44 record two years prior. In fact, between 1994–2001, the Indians' .534 winning percentage in 1997 represents their worst such mark for any season.

"This club won 86 games," Hart said, "I think without a consistent starting rotation throughout the year, and without a consistent bullpen."

Still, the club flaunted its newfound fashion sense all the way to a World Series appearance.

65 The Score

To one generation, Herb Score was a gifted storyteller and broadcaster. To another, he was a talented left-handed pitcher whose career was cut short by injuries and misfortune. He is remembered by some as the hurler who was struck in the eye by a line drive. He is remembered by others as the guy who declared the Indians were headed to the World Series—even though they still needed to record three outs. No matter the perspective on the man, the player, the announcer, Score is widely regarded as an integral piece of Indians lore.

"He was an icon," said Tom Hamilton, his radio play-by-play partner for nearly a decade.

Score was the American League Rookie of the Year in 1955, when he went 16–10 with a 2.85 ERA and tallied 245 strikeouts. He bettered those numbers to 20–9 with a 2.53 ERA and 263 strikeouts the following year. He made the All-Star team in both seasons. But in his fifth start in 1957, tragedy struck.

In the first inning of a contest against the New York Yankees at Cleveland Stadium on May 7, Gil McDougald lined a 2-2 pitch back toward the mound. Score lifted his head, saw the white blur buzzing toward him, attempted to move his glove into position in time, but the baseball sailed past his fingers and drilled him in the right eye. He grabbed at his face, stumbled and dropped to the dirt. At first, he thought his eye popped out of its socket. Blood streamed down his face. He endured severe hemorrhaging in the eye and suffered a swollen retina and a broken nose. He might as well have paid rent at the hospital.

Score typically preferred not to rehash the events of that game and he was adamant that the accident did not trigger the downfall of his career. He was once built up to be the next in line in a slew of legendary Tribe pitchers, following in the footsteps of Bob Feller and Bob Lemon. He eventually returned to the mound in the 1958 season, but arm troubles plagued him and he was never the same. He won only 19 games after 1956 and he pitched his last game before he turned 29.

Score transitioned into a broadcasting career. He called Indians games from 1964–1997.

"The two best mentors I could have ever had were Herb and Mike Hegan," Hamilton said.

When Hamilton joined the fold before the 1990 season, Score wanted to do only five innings of play-by-play and he wanted nothing to do with the first two frames of each game. That was fine with Hamilton.

"Whatever Herb wanted to do," Hamilton said, "he could have done."

66 Vote for Pedro

At some point in the '90s, the Indians had to crack through. The players' strike prevented them from a potential postseason berth in 1994. The Atlanta Braves' stout pitching staff kept them from a title in 1995. The Baltimore Orioles sent them packing in the first round of the 1996 playoffs. The Florida Marlins crushed the city's dreams in the 11th inning of Game 7 of the 1997 World Series. The

New York Yankees, winners of 114 games in the regular season, emerged triumphant against the Tribe in the 1998 American League Championship Series.

The Indians had seen it all by 1999. They had fallen short as the underdog and as the favorite. They had fallen short because of poor pitching, poor hitting, and poor fortune. How long can a franchise remain near the top without winning a championship? The Indians resembled a dynasty, just without the validation.

The Indians, Yankees, Boston Red Sox, and Texas Rangers all qualified for the postseason in 1999. Cleveland had compiled just a 10–22 record against their three American League playoff counterparts, including a 4–8 showing against Boston, its first-round opponent. Still, the Indians seemed poised to make another run at the Fall Classic.

The odds took a turn in the Tribe's favor when Red Sox ace Pedro Martinez left his start in Game 1 because of a strained back. With the dominant right-hander sidelined, the Indians erased a 2–0 deficit and captured a series-opening victory when Travis Fryman delivered a walk-off single with the bases loaded. The Tribe breezed to victory in Game 2 behind their record-setting offense. Harold Baines blasted a three-run home run and Jim Thome clubbed a grand slam in Cleveland's 11–1 win. Boston stormed back with a 9–3 triumph at Fenway Park in Game 3. Dave Burba departed after four scoreless innings because of a strained forearm. Rather than turn to his bullpen, manager Mike Hargrove, aiming to put the series away, summoned scheduled Game 4 starter Jaret Wright. The young righty unraveled and Boston scored nine times over the ensuing three innings, including six times in the seventh.

With Wright unavailable for Game 4 the following night, the Indians turned to Bartolo Colon on three days' rest. That plan fizzled. Boston scored multiple runs in seven of its eight innings at bat, including the first five. The Red Sox had seven runs after two innings, 10 after three, 15 after four and 18 after five en route to a 23–7 romp. Colon did not make it out of the second.

Charles Nagy and Bret Saberhagen both started Game 5 on three days' rest. Martinez warmed up briefly before the game and was deemed available if necessary. He spent the early innings draped in a blue Red Sox jacket, stretching and staying loose in the dugout. Nomar Garciaparra socked a two-run home run to center in the top half of the first, but Jim Thome responded with a two-run shot to center—after Omar Vizquel registered an RBI double—to provide the Indians with a 3–2 advantage. An inning later, Fryman sent Saberhagen to the showers after a two-run shot off the railing perched above the left-field wall.

Boston shaved its deficit to 5–3 in the third and Nagy—after a discussion with Hargrove—intentionally walked Garciaparra to load the bases for Troy O'Leary, who promptly slugged a grand slam to right-center on the first pitch of the at-bat. The Indians responded yet again, as Manny Ramirez contributed an RBI double

Offensive Machine

In 1999, the Indians were an offensive force. They compiled a 97–65 mark in the regular season, despite league-average pitching. Any team that was going to stop them in October needed some talented arms. The Indians scored 6.23 runs per game, nearly a half-run more than any other team. They totaled 1,009 runs, the first team since 1950 to top the 1,000-run plateau and only the seventh overall since the turn of the 20th century. They were shut out only three times all season.

They batted .289 as a team, second-best in baseball. Manny Ramirez hit .333 with 44 home runs, 165 RBIs, and 131 runs scored. Roberto Alomar batted .323 with 24 home runs, 120 RBIs, 138 runs scored, and 37 stolen bases. Jim Thome totaled 33 home runs, 108 RBIs, and 101 runs scored. Omar Vizquel batted .333, swiped 42 bases, and scored 112 runs. Kenny Lofton hit .301, stole 25 bases, and scored 110 runs. Even Richie Sexson clubbed 31 home runs and drove in 116.

and Thome launched another two-run shot to center in the bottom of the third to give the Tribe an 8–7 edge. Once Thome circled the bases and retreated to the dugout, Martinez dug his cleats into the dirt in the bullpen and began warming up.

The Red Sox knotted the game at 8–8 in the top of the fourth and they called upon Martinez in the bottom half of the frame. Martinez had logged a 23–4 record and 2.07 ERA, with 313 strikeouts in 213⅓ innings during the regular season, statistics that earned him his second Cy Young Award. The pain in his back forced him to throw a bevy of curveballs and hampered his command a bit. He still persevered through the final six innings and did not allow a hit.

In the seventh, with first base open, the Indians again walked Garciaparra intentionally. That placed two aboard for O'Leary, who deposited Paul Shuey's first offering into the Boston bullpen in right field. The three-run home run handed the Red Sox an 11–8 lead and provided more than enough backing for Martinez. With two outs and Boston holding a 12–8 advantage in the ninth, Martinez struck out Vizquel on an off-speed pitch that dove toward the dirt. He raised his arms, his left fist clenched and looked toward the sky. Catcher Jason Varitek, lacking sympathy for the pitcher's troublesome back, rushed him and squeezed him tight. The rest of the Red Sox raced toward the mound, circled around Martinez and lifted him in the air as the Indians stared with disbelief from the dugout.

Four days later, the Indians fired Hargrove. It was yet another postseason with dreams unfulfilled.

67 Negotiation Tactics

During his franchise-record 30-game hitting streak in 1997, Sandy Alomar Jr. extended his hot stretch with a home run. Alomar sought ownership of the baseball, but the fan who corralled the prized possession maintained a high selling price. So, while in the dugout, Alomar signed a slew of gear, which the Indians' ballpark operations staff delivered to the fan in exchange for the baseball.

Moments later, rain washed away the game and all of the history recorded in the few innings played. Alomar's home run, technically, never happened.

"I gave away a jersey and all this stuff and then the game got rained out," Alomar said. "I said, 'You have to be kidding me.'"

There is an art to the negotiations that take place when a team attempts to retrieve a baseball of significance from the fan in the stands who receives it. For years, Rik Danburg has been the man at the center of the settlements. In addition to his role as guest services supervisor, he has also served as Cleveland's chief negotiator. A member of the home team's media relations staff will notify the ballpark operations crew, which flags down the fan with the ball. Danburg initiates the bartering process in a sequestered area.

"I'd say 99.9 percent, if not 100 percent, are very obliging," Danburg said, "but my demeanor is very important. I always approach them positively with a smile and say, 'Congratulations on getting that ball.'"

The Indians first offer tickets to an upcoming game and an autographed ball. In rare cases, the club has granted an opportunity to meet the player or watch batting practice on the field. The results can be a mixed bag. Sometimes, a fan can become stubborn.

"They think they're going to get $3,000 season tickets," Danburg said. "They do try for the moon and the stars."

The significance of the baseball in the spotlight certainly plays a role. After all, Mark McGwire's 70th and final long ball of the 1998 season sold for $3 million on the open market. Barry Bonds' record-breaking 756th career home run ball fetched more than $750,000. The league implements specially marked balls for such monumental occasions.

In other instances, there is no telling which baseball is valuable. On June 1, 2012, Tribe closer Chris Perez returned to the bullpen from a bathroom break, picked up a stray baseball and nonchalantly tossed it to a fan in the center-field stands at Progressive Field. He had no idea that second baseman Jason Kipnis had just deposited that baseball into the bullpen for his first career grand slam. Kipnis eventually got the ball back.

After Kipnis' first major league hit—a walk-off single that defeated the Los Angeles Angels of Anaheim on July 25, 2011—Alomar, then the Indians' first-base coach, avoided his team's on-field celebration. Angels right fielder Torii Hunter had scooped up the base hit and tossed the baseball into a sea of frenzied Tribe fans. Alomar, experienced in the act of retrieving milestone baseballs, locked in on the fan that caught Hunter's heave.

"I found three regular balls nearby and traded them for Kipnis' ball," Alomar said. "I chased them down. They were really nice about it. That one was easy."

68 Kenny's Catch

Only the horizontal bar of green padding suffered a worse fate than Baltimore's B.J. Surhoff. Pitcher Paul Shuey, after a sigh of relief, made out just fine. The fans were treated to perhaps the most impressive spectacle they had ever witnessed live. And, of course, the star of the moment, Kenny Lofton, garnered the spotlight he eternally craved.

The Indians clenched a 3–2 lead against the Orioles in the top of the eighth inning at Jacobs Field on August 4, 1996, a sunny, warm Sunday afternoon. Shuey had registered one out in the frame with Rafael Palmeiro aboard via a single. Surhoff worked a 3–0 count before he socked a fastball down the middle deep to center field.

As the ball sailed through the air, Lofton, after giving chase, tiptoed toward the warning track to achieve ideal timing on his eventual jump. He accelerated up into the wall and stuck his right foot onto the padding to prop himself up even higher. With both feet on the ledge, he stretched his right arm over the fence and twisted his body into position to make the catch. As he peered down at Eric Plunk and the rest of his colleagues in the bullpen, the baseball settled into the webbing of his glove. His cleats slipped off the padding, but he landed on both feet, took two quick steps and fired a throw back toward the infield as Palmeiro retreated to first.

The awe-inspiring grab prevented the Orioles from grabbing a 4–3 lead. The Indians would strike for an 11-run eighth to cruise to a 14–2 victory. As the fans showered Lofton with gratitude, he stood in center field, his left hand on his hip, his sunglasses shading the bright sun and he curled his lips and shook his head, as if to—in a tongue-in-cheek manner—act as if it were just another day at the office.

"It's just an instinct play," Lofton said. "It's just something that happens."

Lofton felt that kind of sterling defensive effort—the kind that helped him earn four Gold Glove awards in his career—was his job as a speedy center fielder.

"It has to take an understanding of who you are," Lofton said. "As a person, I knew that was my job and that's what I do. I'm a leadoff hitter. I look at what a leadoff hitter is supposed to do, and that's what I do. I look at what a center fielder is supposed to do, and I do it. I look at what a guy who is considered a speedster on a team is supposed to do."

In 2010, the Indians released a bobblehead that depicted Lofton making the catch. Lofton, clad in his white uniform, is seen scaling a green wall as he reaches over the yellow line to secure the catch.

69 Carnegie and Ontario

In February 1990, Tom Hamilton arrived at Indians spring training in Tucson, Arizona, wide-eyed and naively optimistic.

"I thought in spring training, 'Damn. We're going to win the pennant,'" Hamilton said.

Not exactly.

The Indians had registered only two winning seasons over the previous decade. During that stretch, they never placed better than fifth in the American League East. Herb Score, the former Tribe pitcher and longtime broadcaster whom Hamilton joined in the radio booth, set the rookie announcer straight.

"He said, 'No, we're not,'" Hamilton said.

Then Score offered Hamilton a piece of advice he still reminds himself on a daily basis.

"He goes, 'This is a bad team,'" Hamilton said. "'But that can't have any impact on the broadcast. The record of the ball club can never impact how you prepare for a game or how you broadcast that game. There are too many people depending on you to hear that game and it might be the highlight of their day, listening to an Indians game, and you owe them your very best. It doesn't matter what their record is.'"

Hamilton never expected to last in Cleveland, in his first real job, in the field he selected once he accepted that his dreams of playing professionally were far-fetched. When the Indians first hired him to pair with Score in 1990, Hamilton and his wife, Wendy, purchased a house in Bay Village, Ohio, because homes in the area "had such good resale value."

"You didn't know if you were going to last a year or two years or what," Hamilton said.

Especially given Hamilton's lack of a filter off the air.

"I'm just lucky the booth wasn't miked up during commercials, or my career might have lasted five years," Hamilton said.

His career has persisted much longer than that. The Indians recognized Hamilton on August 1, 2014, for his 25th season as the club's play-by-play voice.

"He's iconic," said team president Mark Shapiro. "He's not just iconic because he's been here a while. He's really good. He's legitimately among the best at what he does."

Hamilton's signature lines resonate with anyone who has tuned into a Tribe game over the last quarter-century.

"And we're underway from the corner of Carnegie and Ontario!"

"Swing and a drive, awayyy back. Gone!"

"Strike! Three! Called!"

"Ballgame!"

Said Shapiro: "He brings the Indians to life."

The Indians posted a 77–85 record in 1990. They did not, to Hamilton's surprise, win the pennant. They sank to 57–105 the following year. Hamilton needed that reality check, though, especially given what lay ahead.

From 1994–2001, the Indians recorded eight consecutive winning campaigns, captured six AL Central crowns and twice reached the World Series.

"I'm lucky that in my first four years, we weren't very good," Hamilton said. "So I had an appreciation for how tough it was for them to get good and begin to win. I wouldn't have had as much of an appreciation for that if I would've been hired in, say, '94. They won from '94 on. But '90, '91, '92, '93, we were not a good team and in '91, it was the worst season in franchise history. So because of that, you have a greater appreciation for what winning meant."

Hamilton can pinpoint a few memories from that era—Kenny Lofton's dash to the plate in Game 6 of the 1995 American League Championship Series, the celebration in Baltimore after the 1997 American League Championship Series, walking around Miami prior to the 1997 World Series—as some of the fondest in his career. He worked with Score and then Mike Hegan, a Cleveland native.

His eyes well up when he reflects upon his most cherished memory, one that unfolded during spring training in 2014. As camp wound down, the Indians and Reds were set to square off one late March afternoon at Goodyear Ballpark, the complex they share in the Arizona desert. Cincinnati was deemed the home team and, originally, the Reds opted to dismiss the designated hitter and play by their National League rules. So, the Indians sent Nick Swisher—scheduled to serve as the DH that day—home. Shortly before the first pitch, however, the Reds granted the Indians permission to use a DH. Tribe skipper Terry Francona opted to pencil Nick

Hamilton—Tom's son, who had been added to the roster that day as an extra—into the starting lineup.

"It was the perfect storm," Hamilton said.

For Hamilton, it was really just perfect.

The Indians had selected Nick in the 35th round of the 2012 first-year player draft. He overcame a hearing impairment and his short stature, played in the College World Series with Kent State, and signed a professional baseball contract. When Hamilton first took the job with the Indians, Nick was two months old. Now here he was, suiting up for the Indians on a balmy spring day with his father still in the booth.

The game was not broadcast on radio that day, but Hamilton's partner, Jim Rosenhaus, provided play-by-play on the webcast on the Indians' website. Hamilton sat beside his colleague and watched his son. As Nick grounded out in his first at-bat, tears streamed down Hamilton's face.

"You couldn't script it any better than that," Hamilton said, choking up. "We'll never forget Tito and the Indians for making that happen."

Hamilton lives for those kinds of moments. He downplayed the notion that 25 years behind the microphone is some sort of landmark occasion. He termed his ascension to a big league radio booth a "long shot." For that, and to the Indians, he remains eternally grateful. They are just relieved his mike has been turned off at the proper times.

After all, Hamilton, a kid who grew up on a dairy farm near Milwaukee, never thought he would last this long in the first place.

"For me, it was like winning the lottery," Hamilton said. "The impossible dream came true."

70 Visit Indians Spring Training

In the middle of a row of straight-laced palm trees beyond the left-field fence at Goodyear Ballpark stands a run-of-the-mill scoreboard. It is not any elaborate video board with showy graphics or fiery displays intended to lure visitors to the venue. The atmosphere and the climate already take care of that. The scoreboard does, however, occasionally post a message that makes many of those in attendance appreciate their surroundings.

Cleveland, Ohio: 29 degrees
Goodyear, Arizona: 75 degrees

Any Cleveland native in search of a reprieve from a harsh winter or longing for the start of the baseball season ought to visit Goodyear. The Indians moved into the facilities in 2009; the Cincinnati Reds, in 2010. The Tribe had spent spring training in Winter Haven, Florida, since 1993. Before that, the club played in Tucson, Arizona.

The setting is serenity. The temperature in Goodyear in February and March typically ranges from 75 to 90 degrees during the day. Clouds are a rarity. Rainfall is foreign.

Goodyear Ballpark sits on a flat strip of land, with the Estrella Mountain range visible in the distance. The surrounding area is newly developed and populated with plenty of restaurants. Both the Indians and the Reds have a complex down the street from the stadium, with multiple practice fields and minor league diamonds.

Before the snow melts away on the streets of Cleveland, the Indians' clubhouse attendants load a pair of semi trucks with player jerseys and pants, exercise machines, bicycles, golf clubs, hundreds of cases of bottled water, and a collection of ballpark mustard. The trucks make a cross-country trip to Goodyear, where the staff completes a two-hour unloading process.

It may take the equipment 30 hours to travel by truck from Cleveland to Arizona, but a fan flying from Ohio can be sitting in the sun at practice in as little as four hours.

71 Living in the Shadow

Since the Indians' glory days in the '90s—a stretch of seasons filled with sellout crowds, household names, and busy October schedules—every Tribe team has had to live in that shadow. Every team has been measured against that standard. Five, 10, and 15 years later, the ballpark welcomes fans donning the jerseys of legends of yesteryear. Long after they hung up their cleats, players such as Albert Belle, Jim Thome, and Kenny Lofton are still represented at the house they once helped morph into a baseball sanctuary.

"Those are players that are worthy of perpetual celebration," said team president Mark Shapiro.

Shapiro added that he hopes those odes to the past are offset or balanced by those who pay homage to the current crop.

"Everybody knew about the Indians in the '90s," said Tribe center fielder Michael Bourn.

And for that, the constant comparisons have made life difficult at times for the organization.

"It continues to be one of our greater challenges as people examine us through the lens of the mid-'90s," Shapiro said. "But I do feel like, as we get further and further away from that, that becomes more of our history and less of our measuring stick."

Still, fans cling to the glory days. When the Indians inducted Omar Vizquel into the team's Hall of Fame on June 21, 2014, Progressive Field hosted a crowd of 40,712—the club's first sellout since Opening Day.

"We'd be foolish not to celebrate those who created some of the greatest memories in the history of this franchise," said Bob DiBiasio, Indians senior vice president of public affairs.

It can be a tad uncomfortable for the players attempting to recreate that bygone era, though.

Said first baseman Nick Swisher: "The '90s are way past us. We just have to go out there and be us."

Said Bourn: "When people try to make comparisons about this team to that team, you can't do that. It's just different."

Pitcher Chris Perez agreed: "I just think it was a great time and they're never going to get over it, which is fine, but at the same time, it's never going to be like that. It's just not. I think they need to get over that, that it's never going to be like it was in the '90s. But they still need to appreciate it, because it's something very special that happened there."

Shapiro has never let it keep him awake at night. He is too busy focusing on the present and the future to toil with the past.

"There is a balance," he said. "We want to celebrate today's team and today's players and we seem to strike that balance."

72 Streak Snappers

It is an achievement that might never be topped, a feat that has stood the test of time, of generations, of eras of baseball that have catered to the skill set required to even consider a chance at such a hallowed mark. Joe DiMaggio's 56-game hitting streak, a major league record and a historical anomaly, did, however, come to an end at Cleveland Stadium.

The Yankees and Indians met on the evening of July 17, 1941. A crowd of 67,468 filed into the massive structure to watch first-place New York battle second-place Cleveland and, more pressing, to witness the possible extension of DiMaggio's streak. Since he delivered an RBI single that scored Phil Rizzuto in his first at-bat of a 13–1 loss to the White Sox on May 15, DiMaggio had notched at least one hit in each contest. The Yankees went 41–13 during the streak (two games ended in a tie because of curfew rules). During the stretch, DiMaggio collected 91 hits, as he batted .408 with a .463 on-base percentage, .717 slugging percentage, 15 home runs, 16 doubles, 55 RBIs, 56 runs scored, and only five strikeouts.

Then, Ken Keltner, a classic case of kryptonite, entered the picture. The Tribe third baseman made a pair of diving stops to keep DiMaggio off the basepaths on July 17. He robbed The

Longest Hitting Streaks

Here are the longest hitting streaks in modern Indians history.

1. Sandy Alomar, 30 games (1997)
2. Hal Trosky, 28 games (1936)
3. Bruce Campbell, 27 games (1938)
   Tris Speaker, 27 games (1916)
5. Casey Blake, 26 games (2007)
6. Matt Williams, 24 games (1997)
7. Mike Hargrove, 23 games (1980)
   Ray Fosse, 23 games (1970)
   Johnny Temple, 23 games (1960)
   Al Rosen, 23 games (1953–1954)
   Dale Mitchell, 23 games (1951)
   Charlie Jamieson, 23 games (1923, 1924)
   Tris Speaker, 23 games (1923)

Yankee Clipper of a hit in the first inning. DiMaggio walked in the fourth and again grounded to Keltner in the seventh. In the eighth, with the bases loaded and New York holding a 4–1 lead, DiMaggio grounded a pitch to Indians shortstop Lou Boudreau, who initiated a 6-4-3 inning-ending, streak-ending double play.

Had the Indians stormed back and forced the game to extra frames, DiMaggio could have had another at-bat. Larry Rosenthal delivered a two-run triple with no outs in the bottom of the ninth, but Hal Trosky grounded out and Soup Campbell bounced one back to the pitcher, who threw Rosenthal out at home. Roy Weatherly grounded out to end the game.

73 Friends Turned Enemies

Omar Vizquel had become so accustomed to absorbing a fastball in his back that when he stepped up to the plate with first base open in 2006, he was amazed he received a pitch to hit from Jose Mesa.

After Vizquel was critical of Mesa's mindset during his appearance in the ninth inning of Game 7 of the 1997 World Series—an outing in which Mesa blew a one-run lead and forced his team to extra innings—the reliever vowed to plunk the shortstop every time he faced him. For years, he kept true to his word.

In his 2002 autobiography, *Omar!: My Life On and Off the Field*, Vizquel wrote: "The eyes of the world were focused on every move we made. Unfortunately, Jose's own eyes were vacant. Completely empty. Nobody home. You could almost see right through him. Jose's first pitch bounced five feet in front of the plate, and as every Cleveland Indians fan knows, things got worse from there. Not long after I looked into his vacant eyes, he blew the save and the Marlins tied the game."

When he learned of Mesa's disgust for the passage—Mesa referred to it as "stupid" and "BS" and said, "If I face him 10 more times, I'll hit him 10 times"—Vizquel lauded the closer's effort in helping guide the Indians to the Fall Classic.

When the Indians played Mesa's Phillies on June 12, 2002, Mesa drilled Vizquel. When they met again in 2006, with Vizquel a member of the Giants and Mesa pitching for the Rockies, the right-hander again struck his former teammate. Mesa merited a four-game suspension for his actions.

"He said he was going to hit me every time he faced me and he did that," Vizquel said.

Vizquel approached the batter's box four months later with Mesa manning the mound. In a 1–1 game, the Giants had a runner on second with one out. A hit-by-pitch would place Vizquel on first and give the Rockies a chance at an inning-ending double play. It made too much sense for it not to happen, especially given Mesa's plunking promise.

Mesa attacked the strike zone instead of his adversary and Vizquel grounded out to second base. The two dueled again a month later, but Vizquel came to the plate with the bases loaded, so Mesa couldn't afford to hit him with a pitch. Vizquel delivered an RBI groundout.

In their final encounter on September 19, 2006, Vizquel stroked an RBI single to right field off Mesa. Vizquel said that's the last time he saw his former locker mate.

"It's so funny, because he was one of my best friends when I was [in Cleveland]," Vizquel said. "We had lockers right next to each other. We lived five minutes away from each other. We fooled around a lot. We cooked together. It was kind of sad that I never got to tell him that I didn't really mean anything bad about what I said in the book or whatever people said about it. It was just a bad incident that turned a detour and he took it in a different way. It's bad that I haven't really talked to him about it."

Of course, that wasn't the only time Vizquel provoked the fiery hurler. Vizquel and Carlos Baerga once went to Sea World, where the shortstop purchased a mini T. rex figure. He placed it in Mesa's locker one day, and when the reliever first saw it, his teammates made a high-pitched shriek, a surprising noise that didn't sit well with him.

"That was the worst thing we could have done," Baerga said. "That guy wanted to kill everybody, especially Omar."

Mesa joined the Mariners in 1999. When Seattle ventured to Cleveland and he entered the game, Vizquel stood atop the dugout steps and made the shrieking sound.

"I said, 'Omar, I don't think he's very happy about that,'" said former catcher Sandy Alomar Jr. "Then when he came up, the next pitch was behind him. He wasn't joking."

74 Colossal Collision

Here came Pete Rose, having rounded third, barreling down the base line, his sight fixated on home plate. There stood Ray Fosse, clad in his chest protector, shin guards, and backward cap, patiently awaiting the throw from center fielder Amos Otis. Rose was not slowing down, not easing up. Fosse was at the mercy of Otis' throw and Rose's aggression. The baseball carried the catcher a few feet up the line, right into Rose's unwavering path. Bam!

It was the 1970 All-Star Game at Riverfront Stadium in Cincinnati. Jim Hickman lined a single to center off of Clyde Wright in the bottom of the 12th inning. Rose, the potential winning run, had been at second base. Cubs manager Leo Durocher, who was coaching third base, followed Rose down the baseline, sprinting toward the plate. Rose collided head-on with Fosse, as their left shoulders met on impact. Rose scored the winning run. Fosse tumbled over in a world of hurt. As Rose's National League teammates filtered onto the field to celebrate with him, the Reds hit machine immediately checked in on Fosse, who stayed down in pain.

Fosse was the Indians' first-ever selection in the amateur draft. In 1965, the organization made him the seventh overall pick. He blossomed into an All-Star five years later, when he finished his first full season with a .307 batting average, 18 home runs, 61 RBIs, and a Gold Glove award. He made the All-Star team and won another Gold Glove in 1971, but his numbers never matched the statistics he registered in the '70 season.

Following the All-Star Game collision, Fosse underwent an X-ray, but it came back negative. He continued to experience pain, but there was no visual evidence to suggest anything was structurally wrong with his shoulder. Still, his production dropped off considerably in the second half of the '70 campaign, when he hit just two of his 18 home runs. He underwent another examination the following year. That X-ray showed that he had a fracture and a separated shoulder, which healed incorrectly. Decades passed and Fosse still could not lift his left arm above his head.

Fosse never made another All-Star team. He never won another Gold Glove. Before the 1973 season, the Indians traded him to Oakland, where he won a pair of World Series titles. He is best remembered, however, for his involvement in a violent collision at home plate, one that decided the 1970 Midsummer Classic. New rules initiated in 2014 barred catchers from blocking the plate and runners from plowing them over.

75 Start of the Franchise

The Cleveland Spiders amassed a 20–134 record in 1899. Twenty wins. One hundred and thirty-four losses. They disbanded after the season. When the American League debuted as a part of Major League Baseball in 1901, the Cleveland Bluebirds, commonly referred to as the Blues for their all-blue uniforms, became the city's professional baseball franchise. It's the same organization known as the Cleveland Indians today.

In the American League's inaugural season, the Blues were joined by the Chicago White Stockings, Detroit Tigers, Boston Americans, Philadelphia Athletics, Baltimore Orioles, Milwaukee Brewers, and Washington Senators.

On April 24, 1901, Cleveland played its first MLB game at Chicago's South Side Park against the White Stockings. Chicago won 8–2. The Blues were not very good; they finished seventh in the American League out of eight teams with a 54–82 record.

On May 23, they scored nine runs with two outs in the ninth inning to top the Senators 14–13 at League Park. After a 4–18 period in May that included an 11-game losing streak and a six-game skid, they pieced together a 15–11 stretch. In fact, streaks were part of their nature. After suffering through a 5–12 stretch in July, they righted the ship with nine wins in 11 contests. They lost 15 of their last 18 games.

They flipped the script in 1902 upon the arrival of nationally renowned second baseman Nap Lajoie. The Indians finished 69–67, good for fifth in the American League standings. By 1903, the team was named the Naps, after Lajoie, the eventual Hall of Famer. For much of the next two decades, the club finished above or near the .500 mark.

Name Game

There are two schools of thought when it comes to how the Indians got their name. The organization contends that the nickname, in part, honors Louis Sockalexis, one of the first Native Americans to play professional baseball. Sockalexis played briefly for the Cleveland Spiders from 1897–1899. On a plaque in Heritage Park at Progressive Field, Sockalexis is commended for his "powerful bat, swiftness on the base paths and his legendary long, accurate throws from the outfield."

The other theory is that the Cleveland franchise wanted to mimic the success achieved by the Boston Braves. That team won the World Series in 1914. In 1915, when the Cleveland franchise changed its name from the Naps, the club had local sportswriters ask fans for nickname ideas. The name Indians was selected.

The team adopted the Indians moniker in 1915. Cleveland's franchise is one of four charter American League clubs—along with Chicago, Boston, and Detroit—to play continuously in one city since the inception of the league in 1901.

76 Manny Being Manny

Manny Ramirez's second career big league game superbly foreshadowed his entire career. In that contest in a mostly deserted Yankee Stadium on September 3, 1993, Ramirez flashed both his hitting potential and his aloofness.

In the second inning, Ramirez struck a rising heater from Melido Perez toward the blue wall in left field. The ball took one bounce off the warning track and disappeared into the seats. Ramirez trotted around first base and cruised toward second. After all, he had hit a ground-rule double, his first major league hit. But he thought he had socked a home run. So he glided past second base and continued without hesitation on to third. Once he reached third, his base coach, Jeff Newman, directed him back to second. His teammates in the visitors' dugout laughed. Carlos Baerga stuck his hands out to make a "stop" signal. Candy Maldonado held up two fingers.

Four innings later, Ramirez redeemed himself. Before a large contingent of family and friends, Ramirez, who attended high school in Manhattan, deposited a Perez offering into the left-field stands. This one did not one-hop its way into the seats. Ramirez tacked on another home run in the eighth inning to finish his second career game 3-for-4 with three extra-base hits, two home runs, and three RBIs.

Ramirez quickly developed into an offensive cornerstone for Cleveland. He finished second in balloting for American League Rookie of the Year in 1994. In his first full season in 1995, he hit .308 with 31 home runs and 107 RBIs. He produced a similar season in 1996, batted .328 in '97, and totaled 45 home runs and 145 RBIs in 1998, including a two-game stretch in which he belted five home runs. In 1999, he hit .333 with 44 home runs and 165 RBIs, the most by any player since Jimmie Foxx in 1938. He proved clutch in the postseason, as well, as he tallied 13 home runs in 52 postseason games with the Tribe.

As the 2000 campaign wore on, the realization set in that Ramirez, an impending free agent, might land a more lucrative contract elsewhere. In his final at-bat of the season, he crushed a home run off the green wall that bordered the picnic area beyond the center-field fence. As soon as his bat made contact with the fastball from Toronto hurler John Frascatore, Ramirez dropped his lumber at home plate and, before he commenced his home run trot, he leisurely walked a few steps as he watched the ball sail out of the stadium. The fans stood and applauded the slugger. They held up signs pleading him to stay and begging ownership to pay him. Slider, the team's furry pink mascot, stood atop the home dugout and bowed to him as he retreated to the bench.

After he posted a .351 average with 38 home runs and 122 RBIs in 2000, he signed an eight-year, $160 million pact with the Boston Red Sox, making him the sport's highest-paid player. The Indians had offered a seven-year deal worth about $119 million.

Ramirez proceeded to round out a career that was met with much critical acclaim. He continued to compile eye-popping statistics and execute bone-headed plays. He won a pair of World Series rings with the Red Sox. He endured trade rumors, made trade demands and was, at one point, traded. He was slapped with suspensions for testing positive for banned substances. He won a batting crown, a home run crown, an RBI title and made 12 All-Star teams. Even after his power display and mental lapse in his second career game, who could have seen it all coming?

77 Nap Time

Nap Lajoie dropped a bunt down the third-base line and raced out of the batter's box. He arrived safely at first base. He repeated the process in his next trip to the plate. And the one after that. And that. Against the St. Louis Browns on the final day of the 1910 season, Lajoie tallied seven bunt base hits, a total reached with a little help from an intentionally lax St. Louis defense.

Lajoie, the heart and soul of the Cleveland franchise, was battling Detroit's Ty Cobb for the American League batting title. The winner was to receive a brand new Chalmers automobile. Lajoie needed a base hit in just about every at-bat of the double header against the

Browns to have a chance at supplanting Cobb atop the leaderboard. The Browns wanted to aid his cause. Lajoie collected the seven bunt singles and a triple to center field. Browns manager Jack O'Connor was fired for instructing his third baseman to play deep enough to permit Lajoie to deposit bunt after bunt in the vacant space.

Lajoie was initially thought to have captured the batting crown, but American League president Ban Johnson eventually declared Cobb the winner by the slimmest of margins. The Chalmers company awarded both players free automobiles.

The second baseman, also known for his defensive prowess, routinely found himself among the American League batting leaders. He logged a .338 average for his career, including a .426 mark in 1901, a .384 mark in 1910, .378 in 1902, and .376 in 1904. He totaled 3,243 hits in his career, 657 of which were doubles. He was one of the most prolific hitters both in his era and in baseball history. For that, he was inducted into the Baseball Hall of Fame in 1937.

Lajoie also served as skipper of the franchise from 1905–1909. He was such an integral part of the organization that the team was called the Cleveland Naps from 1903–1914. Lajoie batted .339 and tallied 2,047 of his hits in 13 years with Cleveland.

78 Off the Scoreboard

Jim Thome's 511-foot majestic shot that bounced out of the ballpark and onto Eagle Avenue is the longest-measured home run in the history of Progressive Field. It might not be the most impressive power display, though. That standard was established by Mark McGwire on April 30, 1997.

McGwire socked an Orel Hershiser offering off of the Budweiser sign on the ballpark scoreboard. The baseball sailed over the 19-foot-high wall in left field. It zipped past the 23 rows of bleacher seats. It struck the red sign near the letter "I" and caromed back into the stands. The two-run home run was estimated at 485 feet. Upon impact with the scoreboard, fans let out oohs and ahhs. Some applauded McGwire for the feat.

"It was still going up when it hit it," said Jason Giambi, a member of that Athletics team. "I remember distinctly watching it. It was pretty unbelievable."

Giambi estimated that, had it not been for the scoreboard, the baseball would have landed on the roof of a parking garage that sits adjacent to the ballpark.

"It's one of the hardest balls I've ever seen hit," Giambi said.

The swat provided McGwire's Oakland Athletics with a 5–2 lead in the third inning. At the time, it was the longest home run in ballpark history, eclipsing Juan Gonzalez's 460-foot blast in July 1994.

Powerful People

The following Indians players hit 40 or more home runs in a season.

52: Jim Thome (2002)
50: Albert Belle (1995)
49: Jim Thome (2001)
48: Albert Belle (1996)
45: Manny Ramirez (1998)
44: Manny Ramirez (1999)
43: Al Rosen (1953)
42: Travis Hafner (2006)
42: Rocky Colavito (1959)
42: Hal Trosky (1936)
41: Rocky Colavito (1958)
40: Jim Thome (1997)

"I can't believe that a man hit a ball that far," one of the Athletics' broadcasters quipped.

McGwire and fellow A's slugger Jose Canseco had spent batting practice targeting the scoreboard, but neither hitter was able to dent the structure. Hershiser paced around the mound before stepping back onto the rubber and taking a deep breath. McGwire would tack on a go-ahead home run to lead off the 10th inning. The A's won the game, 11–9.

79 Red to Toe

The Indians have cycled through plenty of uniform designs in their lengthy history. No team jersey catches the eye, for better or for worse, than the club's all-red, top-to-bottom get-up in the mid-1970s. The uniforms made players look like tomatoes. The red tops carried white trim, with "Indians" sprawled out across the chest in capital letters. The pants, which would make any fashion designer sick to his or her stomach, made the whole ensemble look like a onesie. The Indians brought back the outfit for one night on June 11, 2004, against, appropriately, the Cincinnati Reds. CC Sabathia, who started the game for the Tribe, resembled a big red apple.

Not all Tribe uniforms have been so eye-popping. The original jerseys, when the team was known as the Cleveland Naps, were white and bore a script C and a blue collar. During that era, they also sported striped uniforms with "Cleveland" spelled out on the tops. In 1921, a year after the team captured its first title, the team wore white jerseys with "World Champions" displayed on the fronts.

In 1948, the year of the franchise's second championship, the team adopted a look similar to the one it brought back nearly five decades later. The white home uniforms carried a script red "Indians" name on the front with a Chief Wahoo logo on the sleeve. On the gray road uniforms, "Cleveland" was written out in red block letters.

At a couple points in team history, the club has tried out a sleeveless approach. In 1963 and 2005, the Indians instituted white and grey jerseys cut off at the shoulders, with, from the player's

Buddy Bell, clothed in the memorable all-red Indians uniform of the 1970s.

perspective, Chief Wahoo on the left side of the chest and his number on the right.

The franchise stuck with the block lettering approach in the '70s and '80s, though the all-red uniforms fizzled out rather quickly. The team added a blue top and reinvented the color scheme on its home uniforms in the late '80s, jerseys that were prevalent in the movie "Major League." Once the club moved into Jacobs Field in 1994, the Indians donned newer versions of the uniforms the club wore in 1948. The home jerseys were white with red trim and a script "Indians" on the front. The club also had matching gray and blue uniforms.

Fifteen years later, the team returned the gray road uniforms with block lettering and added an alternate cream home jersey with red trim for weekend games at Progressive Field. On August 30, 2014, as part of a throwback night at Kauffman Stadium in Kansas City, the Indians and Royals wore uniforms from the 1974 season. Fortunately for the Indians, that meant the snazzy red tops, but not the abominable red bottoms.

80 Sunk by the Sun

Kansas City catcher Paul Phillips sent Bob Howry's offering high into the Sunday afternoon sky, one as blue and pristine as the ocean. The baseball hung up in the bright sun. Grady Sizemore camped under where he thought it was headed. He waited for it to return to sight.

By the time it did, it was too late.

When gravity pulled the ball back toward the earth, Sizemore never saw it. It ricocheted off Sizemore's leg and landed on the ground, Phillips raced into second base with a double and Angel Berroa scored the game-winning run from second. It was a decisive miscue, an unfortunate gaffe that cost the Indians the series finale in Kansas City. The Tribe had entered the matinee with 17 wins in their last 19 games, but they could not afford to drop that one to the last-place Royals.

It was September 25, 2005. Time was running out. The surging Indians had no time to waste, no affordable ground to lose.

The Indians hovered around the .500 mark until the middle of June. They swiftly fell 10 games behind the scorching-hot Chicago White Sox. Ozzie Guillen's club sprinted to a 24–7 start. By late June, they stood at 50–22.

Following their victory on August 1, the White Sox gripped a 15-game lead over the Indians in the American League Central. Despite a seven-game skid in mid-August, they still held a 9½ -game lead on the morning of September 8. Then, the Indians caught fire. Cleveland spun winning streaks of seven, six, and four games before cruising into the series finale at Kauffman Stadium. That day, the

Choke Artist

On the last day of the 2005 regular season, as the Chicago White Sox put the finishing touches on the Indians' final-week collapse, Ozzie Guillen rubbed salt in the wound. Chicago's skipper was photographed clutching his own neck with his hands, making a choking sign.

Guillen claimed he was just ribbing a few fans in the stands at Jacobs Field, but even if that were the case, his timing was poor. The Indians dropped six of their final seven games, as they lost their grip on the Wild Card lead and missed out on a postseason berth. Guillen's White Sox, meanwhile, captured the American League Central crown with a 99–63 record, following a three-game sweep of the Tribe to cap the regular-season slate. The White Sox proceeded to top the Houston Astros in four games to win the World Series. They lost only one game during the entire postseason.

Indians scored three times in the top of the first inning. The Royals roared back, however, and the Tribe needed an RBI groundout by Casey Blake in the top of the ninth to tie the contest, 4–4.

Berroa opened the bottom of the ninth with a single to left. Joe McEwing followed with a sacrifice bunt. Then, Phillips called upon a shining star. The sun answered the prayer.

After the ball caromed off his lower limb, Sizemore seethed in frustration before picking it up and chucking it back toward the infield. He admitted he took more time than he should have, though his manager, Eric Wedge, surmised that any expediting of the process would not have come quickly enough to nab Berroa at the plate.

The Sunday letdown seemed to send the Tribe into a tailspin. Entering that tilt, the Indians had narrowed their deficit to 1½ games in the division. They sat 1½ games ahead of the Boston Red Sox and New York Yankees in the American League Wild Card chase. The loss to the Royals tacked on a game to their division deficit and shaved a game off of their Wild Card lead. They had a three-game set with bottom-dwelling Tampa Bay and a three-game set with Chicago to close out the regular season. They could not afford any more slip-ups.

The Devil Rays claimed the series opener 5–4. The following day, Tampa Bay trotted out Seth McClung, who entered with a 6–11 record and 7.11 ERA and who had posted an 0–3 record and 16.39 ERA in his previous three starts, which lasted a total of 9⅓ innings. Naturally, McClung blanked the Indians for eight innings in a 1–0 Devil Rays triumph. Cleveland salvaged the series finale, but the Indians were fading fast.

The White Sox swept away the Tribe at Jacobs Field over the final weekend. They won the three contests by a combined four runs. The Indians dropped six of their final seven games, starting with the sun-splashed setback in Kansas City. Despite 93 wins, they finished six games behind the White Sox in the division and two games behind both the Yankees and Red Sox.

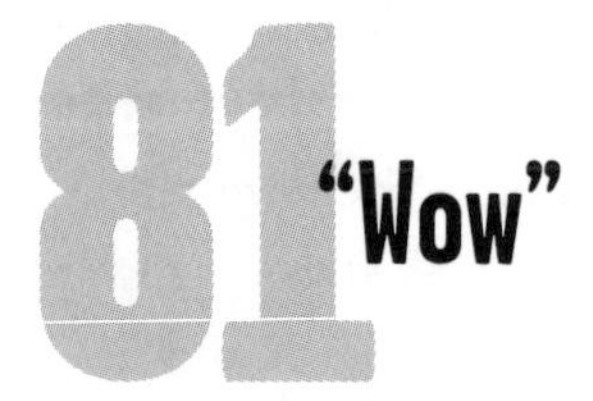

81 "Wow"

Dennis Eckersley did not look defeated or frustrated or disappointed. He simply appeared astonished. More than anything, he seemed impressed.

The Indians selected Eckersley in the third round of the 1972 amateur draft. He spent his first three big league seasons with Cleveland. After more than a decade as a major league starter, he transitioned to the back end of Oakland's bullpen under Tony La Russa in the late '80s. He rattled off a few years in which he recorded eye-popping stat lines, which garnered him the American League Most Valuable Player and Cy Young Awards in 1992.

By 1995, Eckersley, a 2004 Hall of Fame inductee, had turned 40 and a bit of regression had set in, though he was still effective and still owned the closer's role in Oakland. He entered the game at Jacobs Field on July 16, 1995, in the bottom of the 12th. The Athletics held a 4–3 lead. Kenny Lofton stood on second base with two outs when 23-year-old right fielder Manny Ramirez approached the batter's box. On the seventh pitch of the at-bat, after Ramirez had fouled off several offerings from Eckersley, the slugger drove a 2-2 pitch halfway up the bleachers in left field. The walk-off home run handed the first-place Indians a 5–4 victory and a four-game sweep of the A's.

"This place was rocking all the time," said Jason Giambi, a rookie on that Athletics team. "It was so hard to take the crowd out of it here. No matter how many runs you put up, as soon as they got one runner on, the crowd started getting back into it. It was such a home-field advantage. That's what I remember as a player coming here. It was unbelievable."

After Eckersley followed through with his high leg kick and delivered the fastball on the inner half of the plate, the right-hander watched the ball sail into the seats. He walked off the mound and toward Oakland's dugout, unable to hold back a sheepish grin, as though he could not believe what had happened. He then mouthed the word "Wow," a fitting bit of diction to describe both Ramirez's blast and the dominance the '95 Indians displayed.

"When he hit it, he knew it," Indians radio announcer Herb Score said on the broadcast. "He just stood at home plate and watched it."

It marked Ramirez's third consecutive game with a home run. Earlier in the week, he made his first career All-Star Game appearance. The Indians moved to an unthinkable 50–21 with the win, as they increased their lead over the Kansas City Royals and Milwaukee Brewers in the American League Central to a remarkable 14½ games. Wow, indeed.

82 Attend Both Parts of the Battle of Ohio

Progressive Field and Great American Ball Park are separated by about a 250-mile stretch of I-71. It is a four-hour trip from Carnegie Avenue to Joe Nuxhall Way, with Columbus situated directly in the middle and little else to distract travelers along the way. There are miles and miles of farmland. There are often miles and miles of construction, too. At one point, there is a cheese barn. At another, there is a large outlet mall.

Since 1997, the Indians and Reds have tussled during interleague play in what is dubbed the Battle of Ohio. The two franchises boast as much history and tradition as any two organizations in the league. Cincinnati joined the National League in 1890 after becoming a charter member of the American Association in 1882. Cleveland joined the American League in 1901 as the Blues. The teams have never dueled in the postseason, and had never played during the regular season until 1997.

From 1989–1996, the teams competed for the Ohio Cup in an annual preseason exhibition played at Cooper Stadium in the capital of the Buckeye State. The Indians claimed six of the eight contests before Major League Baseball instituted interleague play into the regular-season format. On June 16, 1997, the Indians and Reds squared off at Jacobs Field for the first time in front of a sold-out crowd of 42,961. Orel Hershiser struck out Deion Sanders to commence the regular-season edition of the Buckeye Series. Cleveland designated hitter Kevin Seitzer logged the series' first hit with a first-inning double to right. Manny Ramirez notched the series' first home run with a deep fly to right in the ninth inning off Jeff Shaw. The Reds captured the first ever victory, 4–1.

The teams played three times in 1997, 1998, and 2003. They did not meet in 2002. They played six times—a three-game series in each city—in the other years until 2013, when they began an annual four-game set, with two contests played in each location. Through the 2014 campaign, the Indians led the overall series 45–44.

83 Sibling Rivalry

During the twilight of his career, Sandy Alomar Sr. was often flanked by his two sons in the Texas Rangers clubhouse, the dugout or anywhere else he roamed. Not long after he retired, his sons, Sandy Jr. and Roberto, began their careers in professional baseball.

Little Sandy signed with the San Diego Padres as a 17-year-old in 1983. His brother followed suit. Robbie signed with the organization 11 days after his 17th birthday in 1985. They briefly played together in San Diego. Robbie spent his first three big league seasons with the club before being traded to Toronto. Sandy made two short cameos with the Padres before being dealt to Cleveland.

A passion for baseball has long been rooted in the Alomar lineage. The brothers' uncles, cousins and their father all dabbled in baseball at one level or another. Sandy Sr. wreaked havoc on the big league base paths for 15 years.

The brotherly rivalry reached the limelight in 1996, when Roberto's Baltimore Orioles squared off against Sandy's Indians in the American League Division Series.

"My mom would always go nuts when I played against Robbie in the postseason," Sandy said.

In Game 4, Roberto launched a Jose Mesa pitch over the Jacobs Field fence for a game-winning home run. With the victory, Baltimore advanced to the American League Championship Series and Cleveland went home, having fallen short of a second straight World Series appearance. Sandy's game-tying home run in Game 4 of the 1997 American League Division Series salvaged the Indians' season and permitted the club to advance to face Roberto's Orioles in the American League Championship Series. This time, Sandy was the last Alomar standing, as the Tribe proceeded to the World Series following a six-game series win.

"There's only going to be one winner and one loser," Roberto said. "It was great, but it was tough. As a brother, that's the test that you have."

The brothers joined forces in 1999 after Roberto signed a four-year pact with the Indians. Luring him to Cleveland was the club's No. 1 offseason priority. At last, the entire Alomar clan again had one unified allegiance. Roberto was named an All-Star and won a Gold Glove Award in each of his three seasons in Cleveland before he was traded to the New York Mets.

In 2011, Roberto was inducted into the Baseball Hall of Fame. He was joined in the 2011 Cooperstown class by Bert Blyleven, who played with Sandy Sr. and got to know the young Alomar boys in Texas.

"It was always a good competition and a lot of fun to play against him," Sandy said. "But it was a lot more fun when we played together. That way you get to root for him, not against him. He was such a good player that you would want on your team—he could steal, he had all these abilities. But it was always fun competing against your brother and with your brother."

So which brother pays for dinner?

"He does," Sandy said, "because he made more money than I did. He's the Hall of Famer. He has to take care of it."

"I like to take care of my big brother," Roberto said. "He took care of me when I was young."

84 Catch-22

Nick Swisher only had so much effort left to offer. Grady Sizemore's long ball was not going to be retrieved on the field of play, anyway. By the time the Indians scored their 14th run of the second inning on an unseasonably balmy Saturday afternoon at a brand new Yankee Stadium on April 18, 2009, Swisher was beat. So, too, were the Yankees, but the Indians were not done piling on.

The unforgettable inning started with the most meager, unimposing hit. It ended with back-to-back booming blasts. Travis Hafner started the procession with a weak dribbler to third base for a single. Jhonny Peralta lined a single to left. Shin-Soo Choo golfed a three-run home run into the visitor's bullpen in left-center to erase the Yankees' 2–0 lead. 3–2.

After Ryan Garko popped out in foul territory behind the plate and Ben Francisco doubled to left, Asdrubal Cabrera brought home a run with a single up the middle that nearly removed pitcher Chien-Ming Wang's shoelaces. 4–2.

Sizemore and Mark DeRosa followed with consecutive doubles to right field. 6–2.

DeRosa had to lunge at Wang's offering outside of the zone to make contact and yet he still poked the pitch off the wall. The ball bounced off a bright yellow advertisement and then trickled back onto the outfield grass as Swisher banged his back against the padding and two runs scored. Victor Martinez laced a one-hop liner to right to plate DeRosa and Wang hit the showers. 7–2.

Hafner and Peralta then greeted rookie Anthony Claggett with consecutive doubles to center. Peralta's base knock, over the head of center fielder Brett Gardner, scored a pair. 9–2.

Choo walked, Garko singled to load the bases and Francisco struck out. Cabrera did not. The Tribe shortstop lifted a fastball into the first row of seats in right field, as Swisher made a futile leap at the wall. 13–2.

Sizemore followed the grand slam with a solo shot, one Swisher had no chance at catching. The Yankees right fielder took a few steps and watched the ball sail out of play. 14–2.

A Chance at a Seven-Hit Game

As Coco Crisp strolled to the batter's box, Omar Vizquel gathered his essentials and headed out of the dugout toward the on-deck circle at Yankee Stadium. Victor Martinez stopped Vizquel in his tracks and committed a cardinal sin.

"He grabbed me by the chest," Vizquel said, "and he said, 'Hey do you realize that you have a chance to go 7-for-7?'"

It was the final day of August in 2004. The Indians entered the contest with a .500 record. The Yankees stood atop the American League East. Cleveland blanked the Yankees 22–0, matching the league's most lopsided shutout since 1900.

Vizquel singled to right in his first trip to the plate. In his second at-bat, he plated Ronnie Belliard with another base knock to right. He approached the plate for the third time in the third inning and brought home a pair of runs with a double to right. He tallied his fourth hit with a fifth-inning single to left. In the sixth, he scored Crisp with a double to left. He established a career high with his sixth hit on an eighth-inning single up the middle.

The Indians' shortstop became the 59th big leaguer since 1900 to register six hits in a nine-inning game. Only Rennie Stennett, a second baseman for the Pirates, had notched seven hits in a nine-inning affair. He went 7-for-7 in Pittsburgh's 22–0 shellacking of the Chicago Cubs on September 16, 1975.

So, Vizquel stepped in against Esteban Loaiza with the Tribe ahead, 19-0, and Crisp on first base. He couldn't shake Martinez's unintentionally flustering encouragement. Vizquel flied out to short right field. He finished 6-for-7.

"It just completely broke my concentration," Vizquel said, laughing.

When Claggett fanned DeRosa for the third out, it ended a 14-run frame, one that included 13 hits, a walk, a wild pitch, five doubles, and three home runs. The 14 runs were the most ever scored in the second inning of a major league game. The 13 hits were the most ever surrendered by Yankees pitching in one inning. The Indians razzed each other when someone made an out. They shuddered at the horror of what it must have been like to be playing defense during the onslaught.

And they were not finished.

Garko tacked on an RBI single in the third. DeRosa did the same in the fourth and he and Martinez joined forces on back-to-back home runs in the fifth. Hafner launched a solo shot in the eighth and Trevor Crowe completed the scoring with an RBI single in the ninth. All told, the Indians amassed 22 runs on 25 hits and six walks in a 22–4 shellacking of the Yankees. It matched the most runs the Yankees had ever yielded at home. It marked the most runs for the Indians in a game since they registered a 22–0 triumph on August 31, 2004. That game, of course, came at the old Yankee Stadium.

Hafner and Martinez were a part of both offensive eruptions. Hafner went 3-for-7 with a home run in the '09 affair. Martinez went 2-for-4 with a home run before being replaced by Kelly Shoppach. Both Hafner and Martinez recorded two hits in the 2004 contest. Hafner clubbed a three-run triple in the first inning to open the scoring. Martinez capped the scoring with a three-run home run in the ninth.

The Indians matched the most lopsided shutout win in modern big league history and supplied the Yankees with their largest loss in franchise history. The Tribe did not mount any 14-run innings, but they scored three in the first, three in the second, three in the third, six in the fifth, one in the sixth, and six in the ninth.

85 Mr. 3,000

The pitch was on the outer half of the plate, but it did not matter. Eddie Murray, hunched over, waving his bat straight up in the air, his knees bent—his back one more than his front—could pull the most wayward offerings through any briefly appearing hole in an infield. So Murray, ever so wise at the ripe old age of 39, twisted his hips and guided Mike Trombley's fastball through the right side of the astroturf at the Metrodome.

First baseman Scott Stahoviak had no chance at it. He broke toward the base in the event that his cohort on the right side, Chuck Knoblauch, could corral the sharp grounder. The second baseman dove—well, bellyflopped—after the ball, but it was out of his reach. Murray glided around the bag and slapped hands with first-base coach Dave Nelson. He had become the 20th player in major league history to collect 3,000 hits, an unwritten automatic qualifier for Baseball Hall of Fame entry.

The Indians came pouring out of the visitor's dugout. They gathered around the veteran and supplied congratulatory slaps and shakes. Murray lifted his helmet and his cap and acknowledged the applauding Minnesota crowd.

Aside from that milestone achievement by an opposing player on June 30, Twins fans did not have much else to cheer for during the 1995 campaign. Their club fell to 17–42 with a 4–1 loss on that Friday night. The Tribe, meanwhile, surged ahead to 41–17 as they enjoyed a level of success they had planned for years to eventually achieve. That blueprint included a sizable leap forward on December 2, 1993, when the organization introduced Murray and Dennis Martinez—a pair of experienced and accomplished veterans—as its latest additions.

Murray had been selected to eight All-Star teams, had won three Gold Glove awards and had finished in the top five in balloting for Most Valuable Player on six occasions. He was coming off a season in which, at the age of 37, he still batted .285 with 27 home runs and 100 RBIs for the New York Mets.

Manager Mike Hargrove inserted Murray into the middle of his lineup during the slugger's three years in Cleveland. Murray spent the majority of his time at designated hitter, though he did play first base on occasion. The switch-hitter clubbed one home run in each of the Indians' postseason series in 1995 and he delivered a walk-off single in Game 3 of the World Series, the franchise's first Fall Classic victory in 47 years. Murray, the third player in baseball history with 500 home runs and 3,000 hits, was inducted into Cooperstown in 2003. The Indians are the only franchise with three players to have notched their 3,000th hit while with the club (Murray, Nap Lajoie, Tris Speaker).

86 Thunderstruck

Andre Thornton's booming bat earned him his nickname. Many pitchers learned, first-hand, that it was a fitting one. When "Thunder" Thornton hit the ball, he hit it hard. And it went far.

The Indians acquired Thornton from the Montreal Expos prior to the 1977 season. He filled a void at first base and general manager Phil Seghi was hoping to cash in on a buy-low investment. Thornton struggled at the plate with the Expos and Chicago Cubs in 1976, but the potential was there. It just needed to be tapped.

Thornton clubbed 28 home runs in his first year with the Tribe. He totaled 33 home runs and 105 RBIs in 1978, 26 home runs and 93 RBIs in 1979, 32 home runs and 116 RBIs in 1982, and 33 home runs and 99 RBIs in 1984. His career seems a bit short-changed, though. His time in Cleveland was marred by on-the-field injury and off-the-field tragedy.

After the 1977 campaign, Thornton, his wife, and their two children were traveling to Pennsylvania for a wedding when an icy road interfered. Their van flipped over. His wife and daughter did not survive the crash.

During spring training in 1980, Thornton suffered a knee injury that required surgery. He missed the entire season. The 1981 season was cut short by a players' strike. Thornton also missed time with a broken thumb.

All told, the powerful slugger tallied 214 of his 253 home runs with the Indians. He earned his way onto two American League All-Star teams. In 2007, he was enshrined in the Indians Hall of Fame alongside Jim Bagby Sr., Mike Garcia, and Charles Nagy—all pitchers, and all guys who were thankful they did not have to face Thornton.

87 No Help Needed

Omar Vizquel's shelf full of Gold Glove awards makes him arguably the greatest defensive player in franchise history. He never turned an unassisted triple play, though. The feat is rarer than a perfect game. Yet, three players in Cleveland's history have completed one, more than any other organization in the league.

On July 19, 1909, Neal Ball turned the first one ever recorded. Facing the Boston Red Sox, Ball, playing for the then-Cleveland

Naps, caught a line drive at shortstop in the second inning, touched second base, and tagged the oncoming runner.

Bill Wambsganss executed the most recognized unassisted triple play of all-time on October 10, 1920. In the fifth inning of Game 5 of the World Series between the Indians and the Brooklyn Robins at League Park, Wambsganss caught a line drive, stepped on second, and tagged an oncoming runner. Wambsganss was later presented with a medal for achieving the feat. He lost the medal while traveling on a train the following year.

Eleven more unassisted triple plays were registered before Asdrubal Cabrera etched his name into history books on May 12, 2008. Cabrera, like Vizquel, was a native of Venezuela and sported a No. 13 jersey.

"The number kind of got lost a couple years after I left Cleveland," Vizquel said, "but then when Asdrubal came, they gave it to him and it was great to see it back on the field."

Cabrera occasionally wore No. 13 in the minors, but when he arrived in the Indians' clubhouse upon his first promotion to the big leagues, that number uniform was hanging in his locker.

"I never asked for No. 13," Cabrera said. "They held that number for me."

Cabrera began his Indians career at second base, since Jhonny Peralta owned the shortstop position. Quickly, however, the slick-fielding Cabrera inherited the shortstop role.

In the fifth inning of a scoreless tie against the Toronto Blue Jays, Cabrera helped southpaw Cliff Lee dodge harm. Toronto had placed a pair of runners—Kevin Mench and Marco Scutaro—on first and second, respectively, to begin the inning. With Lyle Overbay readying for Lee's 1-0 offering, both runners took off. As his bat splintered across the infield, Overbay lined the pitch toward second base, where Cabrera made a diving grab. He lifted his glove high in the air to show second-base umpire Alfonso Marquez that he caught it. He then jogged over and stepped on second base to retire Mench and tagged Scutaro, who had already rounded the bag. Without pause, he continued his trot toward the Tribe dugout. He popped the baseball between his bare right hand and his glove as he grinned.

Cabrera had turned the 14th unassisted triple play in major league history. He was keeping that prized possession. One problem: he didn't. Without thinking, Cabrera tossed the baseball into the stands as he retreated to the dugout.

88 Fifty-Fifty

Albert Belle personified power. His batting stance, which featured him hunched over, his backside sticking out and his bat sitting back, ready to pounce, struck fear into opposing pitchers.

No season better embodied his power potential than the 1995 campaign. That season, Belle became the first player to ever rack up 50 home runs and 50 doubles. He finished the season with a .317 batting average and .401 on-base percentage, leading the league with a .690 slugging percentage, 50 home runs, 52 doubles, 126 RBIs, 377 total bases, and 121 runs scored. He recorded those gaudy numbers in a shortened season, too. Belle played in 143 games, since the start of the season was truncated because of the players' strike.

His 50th and final blast came on the penultimate day of the regular season. His 50th double had come nearly two weeks earlier. With the Saturday afternoon shadows beginning to bear down on Jacobs Field, Belle deposited a fastball from Kansas City hurler Melvin Bunch onto the plaza in left field. The tater tied the game at two. Cleveland would proceed to win 3–2 in 10 innings.

A Grand Gesture

The California Angels, leaders of the American League West, were the hottest team in baseball. They finished the month of July 1995 with a 20–7 record, having outscored their opponents by nearly 100 runs. Amid that scorching stretch, however, they suffered a crushing defeat at Jacobs Field on July 19.

Lee Smith, then the league's all-time career leader in saves, entered in the ninth, with California clutching a 5–3 lead. He served up singles to Wayne Kirby and Omar Vizquel and walked Carlos Baerga to load the bases with one out. Up to the plate stepped Albert Belle, as the crowd began to chant his first name.

On a 1-2 count, Smith hung a breaking ball over the outside part of the plate. Belle stretched his arms and put his supreme strength on display, as he drove the pitch over the center-field fence. The baseball landed among a cluster of picnic tables in the outfield pavilion. Belle's blast marked the first-ever walk-off grand slam in ballpark history.

Belle dropped his bat, watched it sail over the fence, and commenced his home run trot, maintaining a focused, emotionless look on his face. His teammates stood and clapped in the dugout. After he retreated to the bench, Belle stepped back out and acknowledged the fans with a curtain call. He raised his right arm and pumped his fist. Slider, the team's pink, furry mascot, bowed down to Belle while standing atop the dugout. The fans, however, wouldn't cease in their appreciation of Belle's feat. So, the slugger again stepped out of the dugout and, this time, raised both of his arms above his head and pumped his fists.

Belle finished with 31 home runs over the final two months of the season. In 58 games from August 1 to October 1, he batted .350 with an .885 slugging percentage, 31 home runs, 62 RBIs, 23 doubles, and 60 runs scored. Belle, however, finished second in the balloting for American League Most Valuable Player, largely because of his strained relationship with the media. His numbers across the board exceeded those of Boston first baseman Mo

Vaughn, who claimed the hardware. But even Belle could see it coming; he told USA Today, on his chances of winning the award: "It's going to be tough. I'm not really considered a media darling."

Belle trumped Vaughn in batting average (.317 to .300), on-base percentage (.401 to .388), slugging percentage (.690 to .575), runs scored (121 to 98), hits (173 to 165), home runs (50 to 39), and WAR (6.9 to 4.3). Vaughn received 12 first-place votes to Belle's 11. In overall balloting, his 308 voting points eclipsed Belle's 300.

Belle never again achieved the 50/50 feat, though he came close. He also stuffed the stat sheet in 1996, when he totaled 48 home runs, 148 RBIs, and 38 doubles in his final season with the Tribe. For the White Sox in 1998, Belle tallied 48 doubles, 49 home runs, and 152 RBIs. He never captured an MVP award, despite finishing in the top three in the voting for three consecutive years from 1994–1996.

"Albert should have won the MVP that season," said Bob DiBiasio, Indians senior vice president of public affairs, about Belle's 1995 campaign.

89 Experience Opening Day

You never know what you're going to get on Opening Day. You spend six grueling months of the offseason thinking you have a semblance of an idea, but then the first game of the year arrives, and, suddenly, anything can happen. Still, there is always that glimmer of hope that the ensuing six months will be special, no matter how the previous season ended. That is what makes Opening Day so cherished and worth attending.

Of course, in Cleveland, anything really can happen. It could rain. It could snow. The sun could shine. The Indians could win. They could lose. It's a crapshoot.

In 2011, the Chicago White Sox stormed their way to a 14–0 lead in the fourth inning on a brisk afternoon at Progressive Field on the first day of April. What appeared headed toward a historical shellacking turned out to be a relatively close contest. The Indians scored in each of the final four frames to narrow the deficit to 15–10 by the game's ultimate pitch.

In 2007, an unrelenting snowstorm wiped away the Indians' opening series at Jacobs Field against the Seattle Mariners. Paul Byrd had carried a no-hitter into the fifth inning when the flurries started to interfere with the players' eyesight. Tribe Hall of Famer Bob Feller is the only pitcher to twirl an Opening Day no-hitter, but his gem came at Comiskey Park in Chicago in 1940.

The Indians used to draw upwards of 75,000 fans on Opening Day at Cleveland Municipal Stadium. Granted, Progressive Field does not have that kind of seating capacity, but the club sells out its home opener each year at the ballpark. In 2009, a rain delay of three hours and 49 minutes reduced a sellout crowd of 42,473 to a few hundred by the final pitch, which sealed Cleveland's 13–7 loss to the Toronto Blue Jays. The last out was recorded seven hours and 12 minutes after the game's first pitch. The two teams played another marathon three years later.

On April 5, 2012, the clubs played for 16 innings before the Blue Jays left Progressive Field with a 7–4 win. It was the longest opening game in major league history. The Indians and Detroit Tigers held the previous record with a 15-inning affair on April 19, 1960, which was tied with the 15 innings the Washington Senators and Philadelphia Athletics played on Opening Day April 13, 1926

Tribe closer Chris Perez, who was responsible for the game going so long after he surrendered three runs in the ninth inning to blow the Indians' 4–1 lead, joked that "if you're going to break records, you might as well do it on Opening Day."

90 Dynamic Double-Play Duo

They made it look so easy, so effortless. Gloves weren't always required. Neither was eye contact. Ground balls didn't skip through the middle of the Indians' infield from 1999–2001. That was the domain of second baseman Roberto Alomar and shortstop Omar Vizquel. For three years, the Gold Glove award hoarders teamed up to provide the Tribe with perhaps the most dazzling display of defense in franchise history.

They were flashy and flamboyant and resplendent. No baseball trickled past them and into the outfield. They seemed to turn every double play, no matter the degree of difficulty.

"That was the greatest duo I've witnessed, in regard to range, acrobatics and athleticism," said former catcher Sandy Alomar Jr. "It was easy to sit back there and call a game knowing that if the ball was hit on the ground to those guys, a play is going to be made."

Vizquel had already earned Gold Gloves in 1993, 1994, 1995, 1996, 1997, and 1998 before he teamed with Alomar, who had earned Gold Gloves in 1991, 1992, 1993, 1994, 1995, 1996, and 1998. They both garnered the distinction in all three years they played together, from 1999–2001. Combined, they totaled 21 Gold Gloves between them.

"There probably wasn't a better middle infield than those two guys," said Indians second baseman Jason Kipnis. "Definitely from what I've seen, it was unbelievable watching those two."

Vizquel was a stable force at shortstop for the Indians for 11 years, from 1994–2004. Alomar filled a void created when the Tribe traded Carlos Baerga to the New York Mets in 1996. That crater resurfaced when the Indians traded Alomar to the Mets after the 2001 campaign. Over the next 10 seasons, 34 players started a game at second base for the Indians: Ricky Gutierrez, John McDonald, Jolbert Cabrera, Bill Selby, Greg LaRocca, Brandon Phillips, Zach Sorensen, Angel Santos, Ronnie Belliard, Lou Merloni, Alex Cora, Ramon Vazquez, Jose Hernandez, Joe Inglett, Hector Luna, Aaron Boone, Josh Barfield, Mike Rouse, Asdrubal Cabrera, Chris Gomez, Luis Rivas, Jamey Carroll, Jorge Velandia, Tony Graffanino, Luis Valbuena, Mark Grudzielanek, Jason Donald, Anderson Hernandez, Jayson Nix, Drew Sutton, Orlando Cabrera, Adam Everett, Cord Phelps, and Jason Kipnis.

Not only were Vizquel and Alomar stalwarts in the field, but they batted next to each other in the lineup as well, with Vizquel typically in the No. 2 hole and Alomar often slotted third. An All-Star in all three of his seasons in Cleveland, Alomar batted .323 with a .920 OPS, 362 runs scored, and 106 stolen bases with the Tribe. His hits often plated Vizquel, who tallied 297 runs scored from 1999–2001.

91 Spitting Image

The Indians and their six-time All-Star hurler, Sam McDowell, were growing apart. A Cleveland native and graduate of Central Catholic High School, McDowell had only ever pitched for his hometown team. But contract squabbles and unrest paved the way for a parting after the 1971 campaign. On November 29, the Indians dealt "Sudden Sam" to the San Francisco Giants for veteran pitcher Gaylord Perry and shortstop Frank Duffy.

The trade paid off for the Tribe. McDowell fizzled out once he left Cleveland. Perry won the American League Cy Young Award in his first season with the Indians. Perry posted a 24–16 record and 1.92 ERA. His 24 wins and 29 complete games led the league. He totaled 342⅔ innings and pitched into extra frames on eight occasions. Perry finished sixth in the balloting for American League Most Valuable Player.

Of course, any credit given to the right-hander was often slighted by some spitball-based assumption. The spitball was outlawed after the 1920 season. While with the Giants, Perry was one of the prime suspects incessantly accused of doctoring baseballs. Opposing players and managers griped. Umpires checked him up and down, searching for any sign of a lubricant that, when applied to a baseball, could supply the orb with some extra spin and dive. Perry pleaded innocence and ignorance and he was never penalized for the act until the twilight of his career. He did admit in a 1974 autobiography to throwing a spitball, but he claimed at that time that he had given up the trick.

Perry followed up his Cy Young-winning campaign in 1972 with a 19–19 showing in 1973. He returned to All-Star form in 1974, when he compiled a 21–13 record and 2.51 ERA. He won 15 straight decisions over a 17-start span and fell one victory shy of the league record for consecutive wins. Perry finished fourth in voting for the Cy Young Award that season. In 1975, as he approached his 37th birthday, he clashed with new player/manager Frank Robinson and, after recording a 6–9 mark and 3.55 ERA, Perry was dealt to the Texas Rangers that June.

Perry completed his career with 314 wins, a 3.11 ERA, and 3,534 strikeouts. He was elected to the Baseball Hall of Fame in 1991. In his induction speech, he pointed out his daughter, Allison. He said: "When she was a little girl, she would find the writers and would slip to them and say, 'I know where my dad hides his stuff.' And they were all excited and they say, 'Where?' 'He hides it in his garage.'"

92 Bizarre Bartering

Littered throughout baseball history are trades involving peculiar forms of compensation: bats and balls, a team bus, or the cost of a fence repair. Such exchanges were more common in the early days of professional baseball or in the minor leagues. As time wore on, a manager-for-player swap or a goodwill trade, in which a player is sent to another team for next to nothing, became the only abnormal forms of deals completed. Of course, a player cannot just be given away via trade. At least $1 must change hands.

"The rule is you cannot trade a player for nothing," said Indians team president Mark Shapiro. "Even if it has to be a minor league player who's inconsequential or an amount of cash, like $500, there has to be something."

Over time, the Indians have been involved in their share of bizarre forms of bartering. In fact, it started before the Cleveland franchise became the Indians. In 1890, as the tale goes, Cy Young, who proceeded to win a major league-record 511 games, was purchased by the Cleveland Spiders for a few hundred bucks and a suit.

Harry Chiti was traded for himself. On April 26, 1962, the Indians dealt the catcher—whom they had acquired just five months earlier—to the New York Mets for a player to be named later. On June 15, that player turned out to be none other than Chiti. The backstop never played in a major league game with the Indians.

The Namesake of Pitching

Cy Young won more games than any other pitcher in baseball history. He lost more games, started more games, and completed more games than any other pitcher in baseball history, too. His longevity, durability and, of course, ability have gone just about unmatched. Certainly, the sport has changed, as has the way hurlers are handled. Young, however, remains a pitching icon, as evidenced by the award bearing his name that is handed out annually to the top pitcher in each league.

Young, born in eastern Ohio, spent the first nine years of his professional career with the Cleveland Spiders. He routinely logged upwards of 400 innings and won 25-35 games per season. At the tail end of the 19th century, the Spiders had crumbled as an organization and fed their premier talent to the St. Louis Perfectos. The new Cleveland franchise started up in the American League in 1901, but by that time, Young had moved on to St. Louis and then to Boston, where he trimmed his ERA even though he had grown old in the tooth. In his final season with the Red Sox, 1908, a 41-year-old Young posted a 1.26 ERA.

In 1909, the Cleveland Naps acquired Young via trade for Charlie Chech, Jack Ryan, and a sum of cash. Young pitched in Cleveland for two and a half years. The right-hander amassed a 511–316 record during his 22-year career. His 511 wins are 94 more than any other pitcher in baseball history. He pitched in 906 games, including 815 starts. He tallied 749 complete games and 76 shutouts, racking up 7,356 innings and facing 29,565 batters. He is credited with three no-hitters, including one perfect game. The Cy Young Award was created in 1956, the year after his death.

In the middle of the 1960 season, the Indians and trigger-happy general manager Frank Lane swapped manager Joe Gordon with Detroit Tigers manager Jimmy Dykes. Gordon moved on to the Kansas City Athletics the following year. Dykes managed the Indians for one more season.

During the 1994 season, the Indians and Minnesota Twins completed an exchange in which eventual Hall of Fame outfielder

Dave Winfield relocated to Cleveland. Originally, the agreement dictated that the Indians send the Twins a player to be named later. However, that component fizzled when the players' strike commenced. So, the clubs settled on the Indians brass picking up the tab at a dinner between front-office executives of the two organizations. Winfield never got a chance to play with the Indians in 1994, but he appeared in 46 games for them in 1995, when the team reached the World Series.

93 Mental Blauch

Enrique Wilson rounded third base and dashed toward home plate, his arms extended at his sides for balance, like a bird spreading its wings or a gymnast searching for proper balance on the beam. Travis Fryman put his head down and scurried toward third base. Their teammates in the visitor's dugout at Yankee Stadium marveled at what was unfolding on the infield. Those in the stands watched in awe and seethed with frustration as the Tribe took the lead in the 12th inning of Game 2 of the 1998 American League Championship Series.

And Chuck Knoblauch, New York's diminutive second baseman, just stood there, near the first-base line, pleading with umpire Ted Hendry to rule Fryman out at first base.

With Wilson on first in a tie game, Fryman bunted a pitch halfway up the first-base line. Tino Martinez charged the ball, gathered it and threw to Knoblauch, who shifted over to cover the bag. Fryman had been running inside the white lines and, as he crossed the base, Martinez's throw struck him square in the back, between the digits of the red No. 17 that adorned his uniform. Instead of retrieving the ball, which had trickled away, Knoblauch argued. So Wilson kept running. Fryman, too.

"I figured I would keep running until somebody told me to stop," Fryman said after the game, which the Tribe won 4–1.

Knoblauch's teammates shouted at him, directing him to pick up the baseball. Fans did the same. It was too late. Wilson scored all the way from first. Fryman sprinted into third. All on a sacrifice bunt attempt.

Enrique Wilson scores all the way from first on a Travis Fryman sacrifice bunt while Chuck Knoblauch argued with umpires rather than make a play on the ball.

"I was surprised that nobody went after the ball," Fryman said. "All I heard was a safe call. Ordinarily you will get the ball, stop the runners, then argue the play. But I saw the ball run away. I saw our runner continuing to go home. I continued to run. But it surprised me that everybody was standing around looking for a call."

Opinions on the play differed. Crew chief Jim Evans said the call could have gone either way, since it was a bang-bang play at the bag anyway.

"When it is right at the base," Evans said, "then it is a judgment call on whether or not he is within that area."

Yankees manager Joe Torre thought one thing: "He was on the grass. It was so blatant, you know, I don't know what to say. It was a terrible call."

Indians manager Mike Hargrove thought another: "I thought they made the right call. If I was on the other side, I might have a different opinion."

Fryman thought he was safe. Frankly, the Indians did not really care if he was safe or not. There was no call reversal. There was no run removal. The Indians escaped New York with the series tied. Of course, they had Knoblauch to partially thank.

He knew it.

"I screwed up a play and it cost us the game," he said the next day.

Said Torre: "He made a mistake. He overreacted to the umpire and underreacted to the ball."

Hargrove said the Indians did not view the play as a gift, but he noted the importance of capitalizing on such fluky mistakes by the opposition.

"Chuck should have gone after the ball and then argued later," Hargrove said. "I mean, everybody knows that and Chuck knows that. Had he to do it over, I'm sure that he probably would. Why he didn't, I don't know. I really don't know. I'm glad that he didn't."

Kenny Lofton provided the final three-run cushion when he tacked on a two-run single later in the inning.

"Cleveland is a good team and you would have liked for the thing to be clean," Torre said. "Have them beat us clean, and again, they got the other base hit to make it 4–1, no question. But you have got to have better umpiring in there. That just leaves a bad taste and it is bad for baseball."

The day after Game 2, the teams held a workout at Jacobs Field. In the Indians' clubhouse, the TVs were showing a replay of the game. Players and coaches stood and watched as the bizarre play unfolded again.

"Everybody was very happy," Hargrove said. "More focused on the game and the outcome of the game than on Enrique trying to swim to home plate."

94 Turning the Paige

Numbers were always important to Satchel Paige. It was the accuracy of the numbers that was not so critical. And that would surprise anyone who ever saw Paige pitch, because his blazing fastball had pinpoint accuracy almost every time it left his right hand.

Paige made his major league debut at the age of 42. After Paige spent decades pitching all across the country in the Negro Leagues; in semipro ball; in barnstorming exhibitions; and in the Dominican Republic, Puerto Rico, Cuba, and Mexico, Indians owner Bill Veeck signed him to bolster the pitching staff during the stretch run of the 1948 campaign. Even Paige's birth date was shrouded in mystery for a long time, so he downplayed his age when he broke into the majors as the oldest rookie in league history.

He was quoted once as saying: "Age is a question of mind over matter. If you don't mind, it doesn't matter."

Paige was a pioneer of sorts. He attracted large crowds at every venue he pitched. He blew hitters away with his overpowering fastball and, as he grew older, implemented numerous variations of pitches into his repertoire. He faced major league hitters in exhibition games all over the country, often squaring off against Bob Feller and his team of All-Stars. He was known to exaggerate the numbers he racked up while logging all of the innings over all of the years all over the country. Who could dispute him, though, especially after he proved his worth as a wily old veteran in the big leagues?

On a wall in the lower-level tunnel at Progressive Field rests a portrait of Paige, in his windup, with his quote: "Don't look back. Something might be gaining on you." Paige never looked back. He kept moving forward, kept pitching, kept jet-setting.

When Paige joined the Indians in 1948, manager Lou Boudreau used him both as a starter and a reliever. He amassed a 6–1 record and 2.48 ERA over the final three months of the regular season. He made one scoreless appearance in Game 5 of the World Series against the Boston Braves. The Indians captured the championship—their first since 1920—in six games.

Paige pitched for the St. Louis Browns from 1951–1953. On September 25, 1965, Paige tossed three innings for the Kansas City Athletics, as he became the oldest player to appear in a major league game. He was 59 years old and had not pitched in the majors in 12 years. His catcher, Billy Bryan, was 33 years younger than he was at the time. His manager, Haywood Sullivan, was 25 years younger than he was. Paige held the Boston Red Sox scoreless, allowing only one hit: a double to eventual Hall of Famer Carl Yastrzemski. Paige also earned entry to Cooperstown, in 1971.

95 Killer Twin Killings

All season, Roberto Alomar grounded into only nine double plays. He possessed the speed and hitting acumen necessary to avoid such dastardly, momentum-killing happenings.

Alomar turned in yet another magnificent season in 2001. He earned his way onto his 12th consecutive All-Star team, as he batted .336 with 20 home runs, 100 RBIs, 30 stolen bases, 12 triples, and 113 runs scored. And he grounded into only nine double plays all year in 677 trips to the plate.

The Indians amassed 91 wins in 2001, enough to capture their sixth division title in seven years. They had been treading water for four months before they commandeered the top spot in the American League Central. Still, even with a potent offense and experienced remnants of recent World Series teams, the Indians were considerable underdogs against the Seattle Mariners in the American League Division Series.

Lou Piniella's Mariners won a league record-tying 116 games during the regular season. The feat broke the American League record. Though they blew a 14–2 lead against the Tribe on August 5, they still finished 5–2 against Cleveland.

The Indians quickly erased any preconceived notions. They claimed Game 1 5–0 at Safeco Field. Bartolo Colon held Seattle's balanced lineup scoreless for eight innings. The Mariners rebounded two days later in Game 2, as they pounced on Tribe southpaw Chuck Finley for four runs in the first inning. Seattle proceeded to tie the series with a 5–1 triumph.

The third game in the series opened some eyes. The Indians scored eight times in the first three innings en route to a 17-run outburst. Shortstop Omar Vizquel finished a home run short of the cycle and tallied six RBIs. Juan Gonzalez, Kenny Lofton, and Jim Thome all clubbed home runs, as the Indians pounded out 19 hits and took command of the series with their ace, Colon, slated to start Game 4 at Jacobs Field.

Colon logged six scoreless innings and the Indians gripped a 1–0 lead thanks to a Gonzalez solo home run. Things unraveled in the seventh. A pair of walks, a single, and an errant pickoff attempt loaded the bases with no outs. After a force play for the first out, David Bell hit a sacrifice fly to left to tie the game. Ichiro Suzuki and Mark McLemore followed with RBI singles to give Seattle a lead it would not relinquish.

That set up a decisive Game 5, back in the Pacific Northwest. The Indians had an opportunity for an early breakthrough. Vizquel reached on an error in the first inning, but Alomar followed by grounding into a double play. The Mariners scored twice in the second on a two-run single by McLemore. The Indians responded in the third. Lofton plated a run with a single and Vizquel singled to load the bases with one out. But Alomar grounded a ball to third and the Mariners turned another inning-ending double play. After grounding into only nine double plays all season, Alomar had hit into two costly twin killings in two at-bats.

No Indians hitter reached base again until Einar Diaz's two-out single in the eighth. That was the only base runner for the Tribe the rest of the game. Alomar popped out in the sixth and struck out in the ninth. The Indians came within reach of knocking out the regular season titans, but they fell short. It would prove to be Alomar's last game in a Tribe uniform.

96 The Art of Pitching

Cliff Lee was less than thrilled that the Indians omitted him from the 2007 postseason roster. He did not have much of an argument to make, given his struggles throughout the regular season. He did, however, win 46 games over the previous three years. So, after the Tribe came within one game of a trip to the World Series and did so without the southpaw, Lee decided to enter the 2008 campaign with a vengeance.

Lee posted a 5–8 record and a 6.29 ERA in 2007. His shortcomings earned him a demotion to Triple-A Buffalo late in the summer. But he opened the 2008 season with wins in each of his first six starts. In his seventh outing, he tossed nine scoreless frames, but the Indians fell short in extra innings. Nonetheless, he stood at 6–0 with a 0.67 ERA in mid-May. By the end of June, Lee was 11–1 with a 2.34 ERA. He was tabbed to start the All-Star Game, the first Tribe pitcher to do so since Charles Nagy in 1996.

After Lee fell to 11–2 on July 6, he won his next 11 decisions over a 12-start span. He finished the year with a sparkling 22–3 record and a 2.54 ERA. He became the first Cleveland hurler to reach the 20-win plateau since Gaylord Perry in 1974. He won the American League Comeback Player of the Year Award and the American League Cy Young Award, the second straight year a Tribe pitcher took home that honor.

Of course, the Indians needed that kind of season from Lee, since CC Sabathia—the 2007 American League Cy Young Award recipient—was traded in the middle of the 2008 campaign.

Sabathia submitted a banner season in 2007, when he led the American League with 241 innings. He logged a 19–7 record and 3.21 ERA. He became the first Indians pitcher to win the Cy Young Award in 35 years. He was the anchor of a strong rotation that guided the team to its first American League Central crown in six years.

Sabathia and Lee had recorded successful seasons before. Lee's '08 showing may have come as a surprise because of his dismal one in '07, but both his and Sabathia's hallowed seasons did not exactly come out of left field. Not like Corey Kluber's 2014 effort.

The Indians had hoped Kluber could emerge as a middle-of-the-rotation option in 2014. He went 11–5 with a 3.85 ERA in 2013, his first full big league season. In 2014, Kluber went 18-9

Historic, Average Season

In addition to Corey Kluber's feats, the Indians set a number of records in 2014, despite going 85–77 as a team and missing the playoffs.

- Left fielder Michael Brantley became the first player in franchise history with 200 hits, 20 home runs, 20 stolen bases, and 40 doubles in a single season
- Brantley became the first Tribe hitter with 200 hits in a season since Kenny Lofton in 1996
- Only Brantley and Joe Carter have amassed 200 hits, 20 steals, and 20 home runs in a season in team history
- Brantley joined Jacoby Ellsbury, Larry Walker, Ellis Burks, Chuck Klein, and Babe Herman as the only players in baseball history to register a .320 average, 20 home runs, 20 stolen bases, 40 doubles, 90 RBIs, and 200 hits in a season
- Tribe hurlers set a major league record for strikeouts in a season, with 1,450
- The Indians established an American League record for relief appearances in a season (here's hoping the bullpen phone line had unlimited minutes)
- They became the first team in American League history to have four pitchers make at least 70 appearances
- Right-hander Bryan Shaw led all of baseball with 80 appearances, a franchise record

with a 2.44 ERA. In addition, his Cy Young Award-winning season included the following achievements:

- His 269 strikeouts were the sixth-most in a single season in franchise history
- His 18 wins were the most by a Tribe hurler since Lee's 22 in 2008
- His 6.9 WAR was the best mark among American League pitchers
- His 11 double-digit strikeout games were the most by a Cleveland pitcher since Herb Score in 1956
- His 10 starts of seven or more innings, two or fewer earned runs and 10 or more strikeouts were the most in baseball
- He totaled 21 starts with at least eight strikeouts, tied for third-most in team history
- He totaled 26 starts with six or more innings and three or fewer earned runs allowed
- He became one of two pitchers in 10-year span with 60 strikeouts in a month

Kluber went 4–0 with a 2.09 ERA in May, 4–0 with a 1.54 ERA in July, and 5–0 with a 1.12 ERA over his final five starts in September. He tossed a complete-game shutout against the Seattle Mariners on July 30 and needed only 85 pitches. In September, he became the ninth pitcher in baseball history with consecutive starts of 14 or more strikeouts. He finished with 39 punchouts in 23 innings over his last three outings.

"It was an incredible year," said general manager Chris Antonetti. "He was, in our view, the best pitcher in the American League this year. His consistency and consistent dominance was a big part of the reason we were able to win as many games as we did. It's not an accident why that happened. It's because of the work that he's put in."

97 Juan Gone

He left as unceremoniously as anyone could have imagined, the antithesis to how he had arrived four years earlier. In the end, the Indians paid him $600,000 for one three-pitch at-bat and one painful voyage up the first-base line. Juan Gonzalez amassed a sensational stat line with the Indians in 2001. His numbers—a .325 batting average, .590 slugging percentage, 35 home runs, and 140 RBIs—earned him fifth place in balloting for American League Most Valuable Player, gave the Tribe an intimidating force in the cleanup spot, and helped propel the club to its sixth division crown in seven years. His return to the Indians' roster in 2005 did not pan out in the same fashion. It was nearly over in the blink of an eye. Literally.

Back trouble limited Gonzalez to only 33 games during the 2004 season, which he spent with the Kansas City Royals. He became a free agent at the end of the year and signed a one-year contract with Cleveland. He strained his hamstring in spring training and was not activated until late May. Even so, manager Eric Wedge did not hesitate to insert Gonzalez into the No. 4 spot in his lineup upon his return.

The Indians had high hopes in 2005. They finished 80–82 in 2004, a 12-game improvement over the previous season. They had a young offensive core featuring Grady Sizemore, Victor Martinez, and Travis Hafner. Gonzalez was considered to be—if he could stay healthy—a veteran cog that could put the Tribe over the top. But he did not stay healthy.

Gonzalez saw three pitches in 2005. They came at the Metrodome on May 31, when the 35-year-old batted fourth against Minnesota Twins sinkerballer Carlos Silva. On a 1-1 offering,

Gonzalez sent a grounder toward third base. As he hustled down the line, his right hamstring tore from the bone. He had re-aggravated the injury that kept him sidelined for the first two months of the season. His season was over. His major league career was over. After just three pitches, his stay with the Indians had ended.

Gonzalez never again appeared in a big league game. He retired with 434 home runs and two MVP awards to his name. His last full, flourishing season came with the Tribe in 2001. The 2005 club never got to benefit from that long, smooth swing that terrorized opposing pitchers for more than 15 years. Still, the Indians went on to win 93 games. All nine regulars in the starting lineup played at least 137 games, slugged at least 16 home runs, and tallied at least 58 RBIs.

98 Blast Off: Watch Postgame Fireworks

The Indians used to host a fireworks extravaganza at Cleveland Stadium on July 3 each year the team had a home game. The thinking was that each community within the city would hold its own Independence Day celebration on the actual holiday. So, fans would file into the massive structure the day before and watch a fireworks show after the game.

Postgame fireworks shows have become more and more common as time wears on. During the summer months, the Indians blast them off after nearly every Friday and Saturday home game. The organization often dubs its promotion "Rock N' Blast," with a different theme or music selection for each show.

One night, vibrant-colored fireworks will sail through the sky above the scoreboard in left field to a set of tracks by The Beatles.

Another night, it will be the Rolling Stones. Another night, it will be Van Halen. Yet another night, it will be a '90s playlist. The show usually begins about 20 minutes after the final pitch and lasts about 20-25 minutes.

The Indians clear out the left-field bleachers for safety precautions and ask all fans to move closer, to where they have a better view of the show. The club typically draws better-sized crowds on these nights. The fireworks can be seen and heard around downtown Cleveland as well.

99 Atta Boy, Addie

The days on the regular season calendar were dwindling. The American League pennant came down to a three-team race between the Detroit Tigers, the Chicago White Sox, and the Cleveland Naps. Prior to the action on October 2, 1908, the White Sox trailed the Naps by one game in the standings. The Naps sat one-half game behind the Tigers.

That day, League Park played host to a duel between two of the premier pitchers in the sport. Addie Joss toed the rubber for Cleveland. Big Ed Walsh took the hill for Chicago. Both hurlers were eventually inducted into the Baseball Hall of Fame.

Walsh, who led the league that year with 40 wins, 42 complete games, 11 shutouts, and 464 innings pitched, tossed a four-hitter and tallied 15 strikeouts. He surrendered only one unearned run, on a passed ball, but it proved to be the difference. Joss needed only 74 pitches to register the second perfect game in the modern era, the fewest pitches in a perfect game in league history. The effort was not enough to propel the Indians to the World Series; the

Tigers earned the American League berth and lost to the Chicago Cubs in five games. It did, however, serve as a beacon of excellence for Joss' short yet illustrious career.

Joss worked his way from a small hometown in Wisconsin to the Toledo Mud Hens of the Interstate League before his 21st birthday. On April 26, 1902, two weeks after he turned 22, he threw a one-hitter in his major league debut for the Cleveland Bronchos (technically, the Blues, but during the 1902 season, they were widely regarded as the Bronchos). He posted a 17-13 record and 2.77 ERA with 28 complete games and a league-high five shutouts during his rookie campaign. In 1904, he led the league with a 1.59 ERA. He went 27–11 with a 1.83 ERA in 1907 and 24–11 with a 1.16 ERA in 1908.

On April 20, 1910, Joss no-hit the White Sox again, as he became the first pitcher in league history to record a no-no twice against the same team. San Francisco Giants right-hander Tim Lincecum joined him in that regard when he blanked the San Diego Padres for the second time in 2014. Joss' career quickly came to a close, though. An elbow injury derailed his 1910 season. On April 3, 1911, Joss fainted on the field before an exhibition game in Chattanooga, Tenn. Eleven days later, he succumbed to tubercular meningitis. His teammates abandoned their game on April 17 to attend his funeral. That July, a group of American League All-Stars squared off against the Naps in an exhibition created to raise money for Joss' widow and two children. Walter Johnson, Cy Young, Tris Speaker, Ty Cobb and others participated, and the event raised nearly $13,000.

Joss was elected by the Veterans Committee to the Hall of Fame in 1978. He was inducted into the Cleveland Indians Hall of Fame in 2006.

100 Pronk's Cycle

Travis Hafner had the home run. He had the double and the single. All he needed on that August afternoon was a triple and he had the Indians' first cycle in 25 years. Of course, the man nicknamed "Pronk" by Bill Selby for being part project, part donkey was not the most graceful nor speedy runner. He was the furthest thing from fleet of foot. He had one three-bagger in 80 career games entering that matinee at the Metrodome in Minnesota.

Hafner approached the batter's box in the eighth inning and... black.

The power went out. All over the Northeast.

The entire portion of the country experienced a blackout, triggered by a software bug at a prominent energy company. In some areas, the power outage lasted several days. Other places' power returned later that night. Nonetheless, some missed Hafner's attempt at the cycle. Some missed history in the making.

Hafner socked a pitch from veteran James Baldwin into the gap near center field. He put his head down and moved his feet as rapidly as they would go. Somehow, the guy built like an ox galloped around the bases like a gazelle and reached third safely. Not everyone witnessed it live, but it happened. Hafner became the seventh player in franchise history to hit for the cycle.

His career was really just beginning.

He batted .254 with 14 home runs in 91 games that year, his first with the Indians, who acquired him the previous winter from the Texas Rangers for Einar Diaz and Ryan Drese. Hafner had demonstrated some power and ability to hit for average in the minors, but Texas had no place for him, given that he was not much of a fielder and the Rangers had proven players at his potential positions. It did not matter. Hafner hit .311 with 28 home runs, 109 RBIs, and a .993 OPS in his first full season in 2004. He hit .305 with 33 home runs and 108 RBIs and finished fifth in balloting for the American League Most Valuable Player in 2005. He pieced his best year together in 2006, when he totaled 42 home runs and 117 RBIs to go along with 100 walks and a .308 average. The Indians renamed the right-field mezzanine section at Jacobs Field "Pronkville." There were "Pronk Bars" on offer, chocolate candy bars named after the prolific slugger.

His numbers dipped to .266 with 24 home runs and 100 RBIs in 2007, when the Indians came one victory shy of a trip to the World Series. Hafner then started to battle pain in his shoulder, an ailment that would not subside for the duration of his career. The club had signed him to a four-year, $57 million contract extension in 2007. He stuck around in Cleveland through the 2012 campaign, but was a shell of his former self for his final five years with the Tribe. In those five seasons, he played in only 429 games and logged a .259 average with 59 total home runs. The Indians parted ways with Hafner after he hit .228 in 66 contests in 2012. Hafner finished his career in Cleveland with 200 home runs and an .890 OPS.

Sources

Many of the quotations found throughout this book were gathered from personal interviews between these players, coaches and executives and the author. Some were provided specifically for this book. Others were selected from interviews for previous articles written while covering the team. Additional quotes and information came from various sources, which include the following:

Websites

Baseball-reference.com
MLB.com
asapsports.com
Cleveland.com
SABR.org
Bobfellermuseum.org
Actofvaloraward.org
IMDB.com
SI.com
Indians.com
CBSSports.com
Heritagesportsart.com
Baseballhall.org

Newspapers

Cleveland Plain Dealer
Fort Worth Star-Telegram
New York Times
Chicago Tribune

Books

Veeck, Bill, and Ed Linn. *Veeck—As In Wreck: The Autobiography of Bill Veeck* (Chicago: University of Chicago Press, 2001).